VAGUS
NERVE

Learn How to Reduce Inflammation, Prevent
Chronic Illness and Overcome Anxiety, Stress and
Depression, Activating and Stimulating The Most
Important Nerve in Your Body

by Stephen Supran

Table Of Contents

INTRODUCTION

What are the vagus nerves and why are they so important? Simply put, the vagus nerve controls the inner nerve center and manages all your significant institutions. It is the longest ever cranial nerve that starts in the brain behind the ears and connects to all the major organs of the body. It transmits fibers from your brain system to all your visceral organs and is basically the head of your nervous system and transmits nerve impulses to each organ in your body. The term 'vagus' simply means 'wanderer' because it goes from the brain to the reproductive organs and touching everything between them. With regard to the relationship between the mind and body, the vagus nerve is essential as it crosses all significant organs, except the adrenal and thyroid glands.

How often in your daily life do you have to deal with anxiety? This book is for you if you find yourself worried too much, if you become stuck in irrational thoughts or even feel nausea, chest pain and heart palpitations. You can learn a necessary yet beneficial technique to cope naturally with anxiety by stimulating your vagus nerve. A useful method can be used to reduce stress and anxiety everywhere and anywhere: at home, while traveling and inevitably in these horrendous meetings.

The vagus nerve, the most extended cranial nervous system, regulates the inner nervous system. It supervises a wide range of essential functions that communicate motor and sensory impulses to each organ in the body.

The longest cranial nerve is the vagus nerve. It contains motor and sensory fibers and is most widely distributed in the body because it goes through the neck and thorax into the abdomen. It comprises visceral and somatic efferent fibers, special and general efferent visceral fibers.

CHAPTER ONE

Medicine to Stimulate the Vagus Nerve

Simply put, the vagus nerve is the head of your nerve center and controls your significant organs. This is the longest ever cranial that starts right behind the ears in the brain and extends to all the major organs of the body. It sends fibers from your brain system to all your visceral organs; it commands your center and transmits nerve impulses to every organ in your body. The term vagus means wanderer as it travels from the brain to reproductive organs throughout the whole body, touching everything between them. The vagus nerve is monumental when it comes to the connection between mind and body, as it reaches all the significant institutions except the surrenal and thyroid glasses.

This is an essential nerve for each organ with which it is in contact. This helps to control anxiety and brain depression. How we connect with each other is closely related to the vagus nerve, as it connects to nerves that focuses our ears to the spoken language, directs eye contact, and controls speech. This nerve can also influence the proper release of hormones in the body, which maintains the health of our mental and physical systems.

The vagus nerve increases stomach acidity and digestive juice secretion to make digestion in the stomach more comfortable. It can also help you absorb vitamin B12 when activated. If it doesn't work correctly, you should expect severe digestive complications such as IBS, reflux, and colitis, ust to name a few. The issues associated with reflux are caused by a vagus nerve problem because it also affects the esophagus. The esophagus is the small reflection that produces conditions such as reflux and Gerd.

The vagus also helps prevent cardiovascular disease by regulating heart rate and blood pressure. In the liver and the pancreas, this nerve governs the balance of blood glucose and prevents diabetes.

The vagus nerve, when passed through the gallbladder, releases bile, which helps the body absorb toxins and decompose fat. While in the bladder, this nerve facilitates the general operation of the kidney and increases blood flow and thus improves the filtration of the body. When the vagus nerve enters the spleen, activation in all target organs may reduce inflammation. That nerve even has the power to control female fertility and orgasms. A blocked or inactive vagus nerve can lead to disasters in the entire body and mind.

Now that we understand that the vagus nerve is associated with all the major organs and their correct functioning, we are ready to conclude that any mental, or spiritual disorder, illness, or disease can be reversed or even healed by activating and stimulating the vagus nerve. You can also find positive effects on problems like anxiety, headaches, heart conditions, migraines, fibromyalgia, circulation, gut problems, mood disorders, alcohol dependence, memory problems, MS, and cancer.

Vacuum nerve stimulation has been recorded in numerous ways such as music or singing, laughing, yoga, meditation, breathing exercises, general exercise, and sound, to name only a few. Singing and laughing serves to stimulate the muscles in the back of your throat. In general, light exercise and diet raise gut fluids, which have activated the vagus nerve. Regimented yoga practice can also increase nerve activation due to the motions, but meditation and OM-ing also activate the vagus nerve. All these ways of stimulation of the vagus nerve have one thing in common: the echo!

Resonant organ frequency reports worldwide by physicians help vibrate the body back into health and transfuse illnesses and diseases such as PTSD, anxiety, migraines, memory problems, depression, sleep problems, chronic pain, and even cancer. You can really see cancer as a form of disharmony. "We are aware of the profound impact of music and sound on the immune system, which clearly has a lot to do with cancer." In addition, in April 2016, during a study that involved Alzheimer's Disease patients, researchers studied the various stages of the illness, subjecting these patients to 40 hertz sound simulation. With awareness, comprehension, and alertness, they noticed "promising" outcomes. All parts of the brain tend to have the same rate of contact, which is about 40 Hz. And, if you get that loss—if you have too little —the two parts of the brain that want to speak to each other, such as the thalamus and hippocampus, can't keep the short-term memory long- term. Tomatis was said to have successfully treated a wide range of sound illnesses because they were all related to inner ear issues. Some of the problems he has treated successfully were stuttering, depression, ADD, difficulties with concentration, and balance-related disorders.

Another study indicates that the Tomatis approach benefits children with ADD. "The findings showed statistically significant improvements to Tomatis compared with non-Tomatis: the experimental group has shown significant improvements to processing rate, phonological comprehension, phonemic decoding capacity for reading, actions, and auditory attention." Sound is a brilliant application of standard medicine, which stimulates the vagus nerve and promotes the health and vitality of all your organs. Do this through Crystal Chakra Singing Bowls and vibration healing. The "Master Healer" is called clear quartz because it is capable of amplifying, transforming, and transferring energy. When working with quartz crystal bowls, the effects of circulatory, endocrine, and metabolic systems on the organs, tissues, and cells are active. The sounds of the crystals are heard in the ear, feel within the body, activate the vagus nerve to resonate through every core of the Chakra in the body, producing harmony and a rejuvenated body, mind, and spirit.

VAGUS NERVE MAY CONTROL EPILEPSY

Quantum brain cure is based on the medicine of orthomolecular, including amino acids, minerals, vitamins, spices, botanical extracts, herbal remedies, and various alternative treatments. There is no single solution to everybody's recovery. If other solutions have not reached our goals, it is always important to remain open to technology. Vagus nerve stimulation is one option that can be treated after trying nutritional therapy. This is a medical device that is inserted surgically. This system can be implanted by any major medical facility in the USA and Europe for a qualified patient.

The Vagus Nerve Stimulation involves sending a message to the brain by a small medical device with regular, moderate electrical stimulation of the vagus nerve in the arm. No brain activity is involved. A stimulus or rhythm is sent to a pacemaker-like medical device. The vagus nerve is part of the adaptive nervous system, which regulates the involuntary functions of the body.

In cases where anti-epileptic medicines are ineffective or have intolerable side effects, VNS can control epilepsy. In some instances, VNS is useful in stopping seizures.

The medical device implanted is a large, circular battery and is about a silver dollar in size. Cyberonics, Inc. has developed the VNS medical device. The doctor decides the frequency and timing of the device's pulses in accordance with the individual needs of each patient. Without further treatment, the amount of electric stimulation can be adjusted with a programming wall connected to a laptop computer.

The side effects of VNS during therapy may include hoarseness, throat pain, short breathing, short-term and slight choking, altered voice, ear pain, tooth pain and a tingling sensation in the neck. At the implantation site, skin irritation or infection may occur. VNS does not have a harmful effect on the brain. This is a significant operation and should not be taken lightly. This may be the last choice for those with uncontrollable epileptic seizures. Consider all options before you give up seizure control.

How to Use the Vagus Nerve to Deal with Anxiety

Where else in your ordinary life do you have to struggle with depression? If you think you are too worried or are caught in non-stop evil thoughts or even feel chest pain, nausea, and heart palpitations, then this book is for you.

You will learn a primary yet very effective method to cope naturally with anxiety by stimulating your vagus nerve. This effective technique can be used anywhere to relieve stress and anxiety; at home, during car trips, and even at those awful work sessions.

Were you aware that the FDA approved an implanted surgical device that successfully treats depression by stimulating the vagus nerve periodically?

If you don't want to have surgery, you will benefit from the benefits of vagus nerve stimulation by following basic breathing techniques.

What's the vagus nerve, then?

The vagus nerve is the critical element of the parasympathetic nervous system (which can calm you by regulating your relaxation).

It is from the brain stem and goes down into the pharynx, vocal cords, abdomen, neck, lungs, gut, spreading fibers, pulmonary, and glands, which contain anti-stress enzymes and hormones (e.g., vasopressin, acetylcholine, prolactin, oxytocin), influences digestion, metabolic activity and, naturally, the response to relaxation.

The vagus nerve acts as the connection between the mind and the body and is the cable behind your heart's emotions and intestinal stucture. The secret to your state of mind and anxiety is that your parasympathetic system can stimulate relaxing nerve pathways.

This section of the nervous system is not available on-demand, but can be stimulated indirectly with the following:

1. Immersing the face in cold water (diving reflex).
2. Trying to exhale against a closed airway (Valsalva maneuver).
3. You can do this by keeping the mouth closed and pinching your nose as you breathe.

This significantly increases pressure within the chest cavity that stimulates the vague nerve and increases vagal tone-singing and, of course, diaphragmatic respiratory techniques - strengthening this living nervous system can pay great benefits.

Respire with your diaphragm. Now is the time to implement this definition. The first thing you have to do is breathe with your diaphragm. This is the basis for healthy respiration and anxiety relief.

The primary respiratory muscle is the diaphragm. It is shaped like a bell and, if it inhales (or flatters out), it acts as a piston and creates a vacuum on your thoracic cavity so that your lungs can expand and the air gets into it.

This creates pressure on the other section, drives the viscera down and out, and extends the abdomen. This is why proper breathing is called abdominal or belly breathing.

Breathe with the Glottis at the back of your tongue, and when you breathe, it should be partially closed here. You will hear in your throat as you exhale and make a "Hhhh" sound to clean your glasses, but without making the sound.

It's like you're dreaming when you're on the edge of sleep and are about to rumble a little.

You monitor the glottis:

1. Control circulation, inhale as well as exhale,
2. Stimulate the vagus nerve.

Now it's time to use this 8–12 diaphragmatic breathing technique to follow this theory.

2. Inhale through your nose diaphragmatically with your glottis partially shut off, as if you were almost making a "Hhhh" sound to count to 8.
3. Hold your breath for a moment
4. Exhale through your nose (or your mouth) partially with your Glotten shut, like almost making a "Hhhhh" sound for a count of 12.

Practice the exercise. The more effective this technique is, the more you practice.

Finally, when your newly acquired breathing skills becomes a habit, you will find your body continuously operating at a much lower level of stress.

You will also note (or not even know) how your breath reacts to stressful situations; your body is programmed to regulate your breathing automatically, and thus your stresses and anxieties.

One of the ways to cope with anxiety is how to stimulate the vagus nerve by breathing correctly. The vagus nerve reacts as a bridge between mind and body and regulates the relaxation response. You will activate your vagus nerve by using the partially closed diaphragm breathing. Use the wasted time to practice this technique regularly, turn it into a routine, and the results will impress you.

Vagus Nerve Stimulation Treatment to Eliminate Drug Cravings

Suffering to any drug will make the life of a person full of headaches. A person who is addicted to illegal substances can go anyway from spending a fortune to deceiving his own family. But how does addiction force people to put so much at stake and then lose everything? Many things are at stake when coping with the rising addiction problem.

Cravings are a severe problem, which many people suffer when they are trying to get rid of the addictive drug. Ironically, many would have achieved long-periods of sobriety if cravings were not addictive. In addition to being considered a critical obstacle to recovery, desires are also the root cause of improvement.

Complete recovery from addiction only happens if a person is free of cravings. It can be hard for a recovery person to live a drug-free life without constant monitoring of drug cravings, but a recent study published in Memory and learning showed that drug cravings could be effectively treated with the treatment of vagus nerve stimulation (VNS) therapy. During care, patients are taught new behaviors that replace their old addictive drug quest behavior.

Impact of VNS on addiction recovery: The researchers confirmed that VNS therapy helped patients recover from the medicine's maladaptive behavior in the University of Texas study at Dallas. VNS is a major operating procedure in which a system is inserted into a wire threaded with the vagus nerve, that passes from neck to the brain and interacts with the mood controlled area. The tool is as small as a silver dollar and acts as a pacemaker. It works mainly by sending a low pulse of electricity through the vagus nerve that reaches the brain and thus controls appetites and urges.

The technique is accepted by the United States Food and Drugs Administration (FDA), is known to be the potential treatment for post-traumatic stress disorder, medication-resistant depression, and paralysis. The study also showed that VNS facilitates the extinguishing knowledge of drug addiction behavior by reducing cravings and substituting for new drug addiction-related behavior. The elimination of terrible memories and the deletion of drug-seeking memories rely on the same brain substratum. VNS encourages extinction training in our studies and decreases reactions.

Drug-free lives are possible Because drug addicts' emotional and physical pains can be temporarily alleviated by addictive drugs; they will finally deal with the debilitating effects of drug abuse. In addition to having a number of physical and mental problems, many of these individuals are self-destructive and suicidal in nature.

Suffering to any substance can threaten life. A patient can only be assisted by a comprehensive treatment program, including detoxification, pharmaceutical drugs, psychotherapies, and other experiential treatments such as meditation, yoga, etc.

In fact, a holistic recovery plan is equally essential in order to preserve sobriety and control cravings.

Nevertheless, the degree to which medical practitioners may achieve results in medication depends on the clinical characteristics of the patients, which may differ by form, number, length, and method of using the drug (oral or intravenous).

Vagal Nerve Stimulation: Placebo Cure for Depression?

There are no obstacles to depression. It can hit anybody anywhere, anytime. Although drugs, including depressant medications, selective SSRIs, and SNRIs (Serotonin-Norepinephrine reuptake inhibitors) and treatments such as cognitive-behavioral therapy (CBT), speech therapy and group Therapy, are standard treatment, sometimes the patient does not respond to the procedure.

The depressed person then turns to electroconvulsive therapy (ECT) in which electrical impulses are transmitted through the brain under severe mental pressures. Those help to resolve chemical imbalances that have affected mental health. Nevertheless, only ECT offers little relief or temporary relief in extreme circumstances and may lead to a relapse. (VNS) Vagal nerve stimulation therapy is a sought-after treatment for people who do not respond to conventional interventions and is primarily used in managing epileptic seizures.

VNS therapy is understanding the basic concept of VNS. It works on the vagus nerve, the longest cranial nerve in the human body that passes between the neck and thorax and the abdomen. This nerve plays an essential role in the control of main body functions. In the event of changes like increased breathing, the vagus nerve transmits signals to the brain about how to respond. The caregiver uses a pacemaker-like gadget under the neck during VNS therapy, which activates the nerve.

Skepticism about the effects of therapy persisted within the medical community, although the psychiatrist acknowledges that little is known regarding the effectiveness of VNS. In cases of severe depression that does not respond to conventional therapies, he is persuaded that the

21

effect of VNS is not like a placebo. Placebo is triggered instantly and ends quickly, while VNS takes six months to feel its effects.

Depressed patients with medication resistance found that those who received additional VNS along with routine depression treatment had higher response rates than those who rely solely on standard (TAU) treatment. The study carried out by psychiatrist Scott Aaronson also found that VNS had better long term outcomes when used with TAU than for TAU alone.

Commenting on the results of the study, the device's tolerability is excellent, because the recurrent laryngeal nerve (the voice box) leaves the vagus nerve. It indicated that side effects could be managed by momentarily turning it off by holding a magnet.

In addition to speech rush, the treatment also triggers recurrent toxins, respiratory problems, and changes in heart rhythm. It can also cause depression or mania to get worse. Before prescribing bioelectric therapies for depression, caution is therefore required.

New treatments for depression

Some new therapies are available to combat depression. Both are incredibly effective in using conventional therapies to keep the disease under control. Three such medicines are listed below, which engage one's thoughts constructively while maintaining negative thoughts:

1. Art Therapy: you can participate in creative arts even without previous dance or drama experiences. These practices open the mind and body to another world and help you relate to yourself. These help to release all anxiety and thus reduce the symptoms of constant sadness and low humor, which are characteristic of depression.

2. Mindfulness-Therapy: Emotional wellbeing and positive awakening are promoted both by consciousness-based stress reductions (MBSR) and consciousness-based cognitive therapies (MBCT). All treatments are based on the moment without thinking about the past or the future. We allow a person to respond to his own senses and gain a better understanding and control of his thoughts and actions.

3. Eco-therapy: Eco-therapy helps you to connect with nature, as the name implies. Whether it's through nature walks or horticulture, it's based on nature's potential to heal, soothe, and calm.

Depression is the world's leading disability cause and affects more women than men. However, one can lead a quality life with proper medication and treatment. It is essential to seek advice from a licensed physician who can diagnose the disorder and recommend the appropriate treatment.

Turn Your Vagus On for Anxious, Irritable and Trouble Sleeping?

What does irritability, anxiety, indigestion, and insomnia have in common?

You're on the right path when you say pain. Specifically, they are all due to the absence of Vagus activity. No, not Vegas of that kind. This form of the vagus is essential for your health and well-being.

In this chapter, you will learn why it is so necessary and how it can be triggered to help calm your nerves, rest, digest and support the natural healing forces of your body.

Your Vagus nerve binds your back, intestines, and all internal parts of your brain. In fact, it is so prevalent that it has been named the "captain" of your parasympathetic nervous system, the natural stimulation, restoration, and repair team in your brain.

The proper functioning of your Vagus nerve controls chronic inflammation and stops all significant illnesses. It controls the rhythm and maximizes the amplitude of the heart rate, which is essential to the health of the heart. And it means that your lungs breathe deeply in the oxygen to refresh your vital energy.

Your vagus nerve translates vital information from your intestines to your brain, giving you instincts of beneficial or harmful effects. It also allows you to collect memories, so that you recall important information and good intentions.

Finally, your Vagus nerve produces acetylcholine, which counters the adrenaline and cortisol of your stress response and helps your body to calm, sleep, and let go.

So you now have an image of why it is so important to trigger your Vagus nerve.

The problem in our present society is that we are so busy, so hyper-stimulated that we are running under stress almost always, without realizing it. We're so used to pain that we don't know how to relax and not how to do it.

We are hyperactive, rather than following a natural rhythm of action and rest. As a result, we feel guilty if we are not always doing something or get bored if we are not excited and entertained!

As a consequence, fear, irritability, and insomnia are frequent companions. This stops us from staying healthy and leads us to chronic diseases like cancer.

So, how are we able to break this dangerous pattern?

Fortunately, your body is remarkably resilient. It only waits on you to trigger your natural balance–it is as close as a few long, slow breaths away.

The Vagus nerve is activated as you respire slowly and deeply. It sends calming signals that slow down the brain waves and heart rate and activate all the rest of the body's natural relaxation response and repair mechanisms.

Slow deep breathing is therefore essential. But, there's a question. Living in constant stress encourages a fixed, quick, shallow breathing pattern.

Slow deep breathing can therefore take some practice. A quick Deep Breathing Meditation: Lie on your back and close your eyes gently. Place hands on your lower abdomen, one on the top of the other.

When you breathe, let your lower abdomen rise gently, as if it's breathing. As you exhale, let down your lower abdomen to relax, as if it were emptying.

Sit in a gentle rhythm, quickly follow the wind, as your belly rises and falls softly. See if you can't force it, but pay attention just as it happens naturally, quickly, without effort.

When you continue, see if you can note when you start to inhale and continue until you stop naturally. So consider the moment you begin exhaling and follow it through until you pause usually.

Enjoy at least some minutes of this calming rhythm and note how good you feel. If you can, just go ahead and try, so that you see it for yourself.

A quick deep breathing technique can be done once a day to relieve the tension of the day and stress levels accumulated from the past. Every night before sleep, you can do it lying in bed to ready your body for deep rest.

In no time, you will reset the natural balance of your body, and that will translate into a balanced, happy, and peaceful life.

DO YOU KNOW WHERE YOUR VAGUS IS?

Definition of vagus: cranial nerve X vagus (Latin, vagus= wandering), mixed neck and head (lungs, larynx, pulmonary), heart and abdominal viscera, leaving the gastrointestinal tract innervating. The sensory, motor and automatic functions of this mixed nerve are viscera (digestion, glands, heart rate).

Sure, you have one, as we all do, it is a long and wandering nerve that connects the brain and the body's organ. It is the primary nerve. It mediates your heartbeat, digestion, removal, and necessarily all of your body's automatic functions. We also address how the state of your nervous system and immune system operate in relation to health and longevity.

The vagus is directly related to our aging, and it monitors the nervous system and immune system that contribute directly to our health and longevity. When we age, the most significant problems include inflammatory diseases in our bodies, which are directly associated with stress, fast lane life, and unhealthy dietary lifestyles. There also have another part of our bodies that helps us to keep our aging process healthy and active, and keeping it safe is reducing stress and maintaining a completely healthy lifestyle.

What can we do to reduce the vagus and avoid premature aging and to live a happy and long life? It can be done through meditation, chi kong, directed views and yoga; all of them are fun and easy to do and take a few moments out of the day.

They understand wellbeing not as an absence of sickness but as the mechanism through which people maintain a sense of coherence (i.e., a feeling that life is understandable, manageable, and meaningful), of functioning in the face of changes in themselves and their relations with their surroundings.

CHAPTER TWO

What Is Inflammation

For those of you who have sprained a knee and felt the swelling, warmth, and discomfort, the process is called inflammation. But is the general public or fitness instructors very familiar with this disease process? Inflammation is a pervasive part of our lexicon. We read about it and hear it on TV. This section focuses on pathophysiology, defines acute versus chronic inflammation, and defines the final organ harms from chronic inflammation so that the reader is more than a perfunctory study — eventually, a list of prescription medicines and specific natural ways of treating inflammation will be highlighted.

Inflammation is simply a non-specific cell injury response. Trauma, infection, or autoimmune responses may lead to injury. The elaborate process involves white blood cells, vessels of blood, and chemical mediators. For its own defense, the body depends on the inflammatory process. Inflammation, in turn, kills species like viruses and bacteria in order to prevent their replication and spread throughout our tissue. It also reduces the damage of the tissue to a restricted area and prevents the spread of invasive microbes. Inflammation also allows waste to be removed and repair of damaged tissues and organs to take place.

There are two inflammatory elements: cellular and vascular. The cell component includes immune cells called neutrophils and monocytes that are responsible for "eating" the poor by a process called phagocytosis. The cellular part contains bacteria and viruses. These cells are commonly referred to as phagocytes and migrate and adhere to the walls of vessels in the case of acute injury or insult at the site of the damage (a process called marginalization).

In a process called emigration, oppressed cells migrate through the vessel walls to the exact location of the wound or diseased tissue. For neutrophils, it can take six to 24 hours, and for monocytes, it can take 24 to 48 hours. This represents the delay that we see after an acute inflammatory issue. The vascular portion induces vasodilation, blood flow increase, and capillary permeability at the site of the injury.

The supplementary system or plasma proteins that are produced by our body to attract WBCs and degranulate mast cells is yet another component of inflammation. The kinins (as in bradykinin and prostaglandin E) are classified as-3, C-5. The chemicals mediators at the site, responsible for= 2 0 swellings of the diseased tissue, are known for causing pain. Plasma proteins in the group of arachidonic acid contain inflammatory leukotrienes (PGD2, F2, E2, A2 thromboxanes). Anti-inflammatory drugs (NSAID) and cortisone block the receptors of thromboxanes and arachidonic acid to reduce inflammation. This is why Aspirin or Motrin is routinely prescribed when there is an acute injury.

Interferon and Tumor necrosis factor (TNF) are other chemical mediators. Among other things, these chemical mediators are partly responsible for causing fever. Fever is one of the body's viral and bacterial invasion mechanisms. These chemical mediators have been known to react to NSAIDs. That is why they are used in the battle against fever.

Leukocytosis (higher blood counts for WBC), lack of appetite, fever, increase in a deep sleep, weight loss, and fatigue are the consequences of inflammation. With the resolution of inflammation, we see a return to average vascular permeability, edema reduction of tissue swelling as plasma proteins are removed by a lymphatic system, and macrophage phagocytosis eliminates damaged cellular debris.

Chronic inflammation. By definition, the chronic inflammation takes over two weeks, occurs when the invading organization is not wholly destroyed, there is still an alien body or an ongoing irritant, the auto-immune response continues, or tissue destruction is very significant. While the mechanisms of acute inflammation are well known, the pathways of chronic inflammation are much less known and understood in their molecular pathways, mechanisms of dissemination, and disorders. Nevertheless, chronic inflammatory diseases are known to arise from an inadequate immune system that continues to attack our body when it interacts with intensely offending tissues.

Chronic inflammation affects almost every human organ system from your skin to the food (gastrointestinal) system, from the heart and lungs to the brain, joints, and vascular system. The best-known example to the public is rheumatoid arthritis in our knees, periodontal gum disease, lung asthma, and Crohn's bowel disease.

But we also see signs of inflammation at work in other organ systems such as skin psoriasis, multiple neurological system sclerosis, and coronary heart disease. Cancers are another disease that inflammation has a say in; chronic inflammation induces malignant cell shifts, and cancer cells reverse to sustain an inflammatory microenvironment.

Lipid metabolism and inflammation are linked. Studies indicate a correlation between atherosclerosis (hardening of the artery), as low-density cholesterol (LDL-C) induces pro-inflammatory conditions to form plaques on artery walls. This relationship shows the connection between periodontal disease and coronary artery disease.

Bad inflammatory dentures are a risk factor for plaque formation in your coronary arteries. A sedentary lifestyle is known as a risk factor for chronic illness. Lack of practice is related to dysfunction of the immune system, in which inactivity and obesity lead to low-grade systemic inflammatory conditions that encourage diseases. Therefore, many individuals who do not engage in daily exercise are inflamed continuously. Chronic inflammation is detrimental and increases morbidity and mortality.

Traditional western medicine treatment options include anti-inflammatory medications in a number of different types. Sources include NSAIDs previously mentioned for the treatment of osteo and rheumatoid arthritis. NSAIDs are successful in the treatment of pain and inflammation but are affected by some adverse effects of ulcerative and gastro-intestinal bleeding (nephrotoxicity) on the stomach lining.

The effects of cortisone or corticosteroids on appetite, weight gain, and other hormonal axis are also used. They are also involved in mineral loss (osteoporosis) in our skeletal system. The HMG-COA Reductase (statin) class of medicines used to treat high cholesterol has anti-inflammatory properties and is promoted as the primary cardiovascular disease medication for the 21st century; not only in terms of lowering lipids but also in terms of reducing inflammation of the coronary arteries responsible for plaque development.

Inflammation and Alzheimer's disease are even related. Studies have tried to convince the medical community that statin drugs have a role in dementia therapy. Nonetheless, it has become controversial in recent years, and statins have been frustrated as a preventative measure against Alzheimer's disease.

At this point, the U.S. Cardiology College or the American Heart Association/National Heart, Lung and Blood Institute, and most professional societies use recommendations on statin drugs. The pharmaceutical industry, in almost every case, is pushing hard for the average person to have statin medicines prescribed for nearly everyone.

Physicians and pharmaceutical providers are affected by 'evidence-based research' which the manufacturers of these drugs actually endorse. These drug companies would like to see statins put in every municipal water system in the country. Next, science is prejudicial.

These studies are specially selected for publications by the drug companies as they report the results they want. Many "bad" reviews are banned, or a mysterious journal is secret. Furthermore, these drugs are beneficial and have severe side effects. Such medications should only be recommended for patients with acute coronary artery disease (CAD) or extremely elevated lipids or other risk factors, and only after confirmation will the benefits outweigh the risks posed by these medications. In other words, they should not be readily administered.

The same can be argued for the widespread NSAID prescription. Over recent years, the use of COX-2 inhibitors has shown issues with the high incidence of gastrointestinal, respiratory, and renal bleeding attributed to NSAIDs. Cardiac and hepatic activity with specific selective COX-2 inhibitors resulted in Vioxx and Bextra products being removed from the

FDA market. The quest for medicines to reduce chronic inflammation once again is an essential priority for research and a lucrative endeavor for pharmaceutical companies. The industry needs to look carefully for safe and effective drugs and not be impetuous to make a rapid profit.

The use of common herbs would be healthier and more natural ways to control chronic inflammation with fewer side effects. A herb can all be used as a medicament for acute and chronic inflammation, including Arnica, Ginger, Bromelain, Boswellia, Turmeric, and Witch Hazel. For thousands of years, Ayurvedic and traditional Chinese medicine have been using them.

Another way to protect yourself against chronic inflammation is to exercise regularly and improve your health and fitness. Diet is also significant, as research has shown that high diets of saturated fats and carbohydrates are pro-inflammatory. A well balanced low-carb diet eliminates inflammation and decreases it. Not to be overlooked are the many dietary supplements that are considered overly essential for reducing inflammation, but include Vitamin A, Vitamin C, Vitamin D and Vitamin E, vitamin B-12, copper and zinc minerals, to name a few.

Effectively Reduce Inflammation In Your Body

Inflammation is the most common health issues in everyday life. Due to a variety of causes, such a health problem may occur. Nevertheless, there are many ways that you can combat such inflammation in your body, such as a healthy diet and the right supplements. If you are getting soreness in your shape and want to know how to avoid it, you have to bear in mind some essential tips to reduce inflammation.

Eat antioxidant-rich food and stop eating processed foods. One of the most useful means of reducing inflammation in the body is to eat foods rich in antioxidants. Antioxidants improve the body's metabolism and circulation. As a result, they will reduce the inflammation you feel very natural in your body. Some of the rich antioxidant foods to be eaten are strawberries, prunes, raspberries, and blackberries. One best tip to remember is to avoid processed foods. These foods can be a significant barrier if you try to reduce your body's inflammation. This is because there is no high concentration of anti-oxidants in such food items. These include incredibly unhealthy ingredients such as saturated fats, refined carbohydrates, trans-fat, etc. that can increase the inflammation problem of your body. If you want to get rid of inflammation, it should be essential to cut the processed foods off from your diet.

Frequently avoid carbonated drinks and exercise. You really should avoid drinking carbonated beverages dependent on sugar. The best is to drink plenty of water all day long. You will keep your body entirely hydrated if you drink sufficient amounts of water during the day. Digestion becomes very simple as the body remains hydrated. Green tea is an excellent alternative to the carbonated drinks you might consider eating. Regular exercise is also one of the most crucial ways to reduce inflammation in your body, and a proper campaign should be undertaken. When you work out for half an hour or one hour a day, you will naturally lose weight. As a result, you can reduce the pressure you place on your ligaments and joints, leading to less inflammation.

There are many ways to remove inflammation tips that you can take into account to reduce this in your body. Such guidelines are well-known and will guarantee successful results if you follow them carefully.

Best Way To Reduce Inflammation: You are doing more than merely reducing inflammation by discovering the best way to reduce inflammation.

It is essential to understand what inflammation is and what it is supposed to be. It is also necessary to understand what causes excessive inflammation to reduce or eliminate it.

Then you are better on the way to know if inflammation is necessary and when it is a sign that thing has to be altered.

Inflammation after an injury is a natural and healthy symptom. Swelling, pain, and limited movement are formed. This means that you do not further damage and aggravate the injury. The intention is to pause and to allow time for the loss to be repaired.

Many people can afford this luxury, so they use anti-inflammatory medications. While these seem to benefit you in the short term, they hurt you in a long time. By suppressing your immune system, you prevent your body, if left alone, from doing very well.

Chronic injury effects are a popular sequel, especially arthritis.

If you learn to use the natural method of homeopathy to boost immune, you can get the best from both worlds. Homeopathy may heal quickly so that an infection is apparent. And this is achieved by enhancing the immune system.

This is usually called a "win-win" scenario. You win, even if your body isn't different.

Chronic inflammation is entirely different. This is when you produce body over, such as frequent respiratory problems and digestion. Have you ever consumed food that soon afterward provides a lot of phlegm in your throat? This shows that food is not appropriate for your body. This causes inflammation.

Chronic inflammation is usually caused by high animal protein in your diet, arachidonic acid contains animal protein, and it increases the amount of inflammation in your body. The solution to your chronic inflammation can be simply by raising your consumption of animal protein. You may wonder why when someone else in your family eats the same thing but has no inflammation?

Everyone is a person that responds to conditions differently. The answer is to say that one man's meat is another man's poison. Nevertheless, it can also be indicative of a digestive imbalance. And the most supportive people are professional homeopaths to help you relax.

WHAT TO AVOID WHEN REDUCING INFLAMMATION

Inflammation may result in disease, diabetes, and obesity of Alzheimer's. Most shockingly, it can cause heart attacks.

It is, therefore, essential that inflammation is that.

Here are the primary ways of reducing inflammation provided:

- Eat healthy food. The food we eat has many effects on your body's inflammation.

Throughout fruits and vegetables, multivitamins and minerals support the immune system and rebuild the body. It is also important to add essential fatty acids to your diet, such as omega 3. It protects the heart because it is anti-inflammatory. Furthermore, suitable anti-inflammatory substances are olive oil and grapes oil.

- Prevent poor eating. Trans-fat removal is good for the body because it causes inflammation. Avoiding foods that cause allergic reactions and produce excessive fat is also suitable for preventing inflammation in the body.

- Be involved physically. Cut off your waistline and do some workout. Reduce the food you eat and practice daily drills to keep your body healthy. Exercise also to rid yourself of tension and enjoy the outside. Aerobics or other forms of exercise are not necessary; it might be a form of outdoor sport that exercises the joints and keeps the body flexible.

- Get sufficient sleep, but not too much. Too much sleep is so unhealthy that it doesn't get enough. They cause body inflammation. Rest provides the body with time to relax and refresh what it used to be during the day, so it's an excellent way to reduce inflammation.

- Avoid negative practices. Drinking and smoking are extremely harmful to your health. Smoking thus hardens the arteries and increases inflammation. Taking the stomach is terrible because it affects the liver. All vices are bad for the brain and cause body organ decay.

- Remove toxic environmental factors and detoxify the exercise. While toxic elements in the body cannot be fully detoxified, at least twice a year detoxifies the body and helps to reduce inflammation. It is also a great help to remove toxins and allergens from the climate. While exposure to some toxins helps the body develop antibodies, it is better to avoid most of them. Fresh air breathing promotes good health.

Inflammation is caused by the body's toxins and harmful chemicals. They must realize that taking care of ourselves is also the best way to reduce discomfort due to body effects and diseases. It is up to us to seek first care of ourselves in order to fully lead a healthy life in spite of the complicated way our bodies function.

Foods That Reduce Inflammation

Rigidity, Pain, and swelling are only a few symptoms of inflammation. Many things can cause inflammation, allergies, fall, injury, or even acne. Inflammation may also be caused by illnesses such as foin fever, acid reflux, atherosclerosis, heart disease, Alzheimer's disease, irritable bowel syndrome, Parkinson's disease, asthma, cancer, and infections. There are several ways to combat inflammation, medicine, rest, exercise, and operation in extreme cases. For many people who seek natural or therapeutic medications for an anti-inflammatory diet, however, they may be as effective as alternative treatments.

Here is a list of foods to be included in your diet in order to reduce inflammatory symptoms.

Fatty acids Omega-3: Fatty acids Omega-3 helps reduce inflammation, decrease the risk of heart disease and cardiovascular disease, and enhance the functioning of the brain. Naturally, Omega-3 fatty acids occur in cold-water, oily fish, flax seeds, canola, and potato seeds. Salmon has the highest omega-3 levels. Add 2-3 portions of fish per week to raise your fatty acids of omega-3. If you're not a fan of seafood, you might add additional fish oil to your diet.

Citrus fruit: Citrus fruit contains vitamin C that contributes to the development of collagen. Collagen helps blood vessels, tendons, ligaments, and bones to build and repair. Vitamin C is an antioxidant that combats free radicals and inflammation. Oranges, grapefruit, lemon, and lime are included in citrus fruits. The daily doses recommended for women of vitamin C are 75 mg per day and 90 mg for men.

Berries: Berry is filled with potent antioxidants to counter inflammation and damage to the cells. Blueberry, raspberries, strawberries, blackberries, sweet berries, and cherries are types of berries. Add to your healthy diet one part of fresh or frozen berries.

Orange vegetables: Carrots, squash, and sweet potatoes are high in beta-carotene and vitamin A. Both of these compounds, are more readily available when cooked against inflammation. You will dramatically reduce your risk of inflammation by consuming these foods regularly.

Whole grains: Whole grains are three parts, an outer hull, and two inner parts, unlike regular grains. The hull contains the essential nutrients, like the antioxidant vitamin E. Whole grains also help to manage weight, which also helps to reduce inflammatory pain. Types of whole grains include wheat heads, rice, oatmeal, and bulgur.

Onion and their cousins garlic, leek, and scallions help to combat inflammation and pain. These vegetables contain a compound of quercetin that blocks the chemicals leading to inflammation. Onions and garlic are very pungent and can be fried or sautéed before consumption.

Ginger: Ginger contains anti-inflammatory compounds. Ginger is very flexible, and it can either be added or drunk in tea to foods like a seasoning. When you choose ginger supplements, you can also reduce inflammation. Always make sure that ginger does not counteract any drugs you are taking already.

Olive oil: Olive oil contains anti-inflammatory compounds, particularly extra virgin olive oil, which helps to reduce inflammation by inhibiting its ability to flourish. Substitute margarine and butter with an olive oil tablespoon. Don't overdo it, though, as olive oil is very rich in calories.

Pineapple: Pineapple is high in bromelain and vitamin C. Both are important for reducing discomfort and inflammatory swelling. Pineapple is versatile and can be added to several dishes in the way you can eat it. Bromelain is used in additional types as well.

Because of the complex carbohydrates called fucoidan, Kelp has anti-inflammatory properties. It is also high in fiber and causes inadequate digestion and weight loss. Spinach is full of vitamins and minerals as well as antioxidants, including carotenoids and vitamin E. Inflammation is minimized by the elimination of free radicals.

Broccoli: Broccoli contains vitamin C and calcium and its close relative cauliflowers. Its antioxidants act as an anti-inflammatory agent.

FIVE FOODS THAT FIGHT

Several factors cause inflammation in the body. Tissue damage can sometimes play a part, and sometimes inflammation is caused by infection. Genetics plays a vital role in families as illnesses such as rheumatoid arthritis are transmitted. Diet and germs can also lead to inflammation, because the food you eat and germs and contaminants may cause flare-ups in your setting.

Some foods can also cause inflammation, such as caffeine, other fats, and fatty acids. In order to naturally reduce inflammation, junk food, fast food, and sugary drinks and sweets must be avoided.

You want to have the kind of food that is safer for your overall health in order to reduce the likelihood of inflammation. Such foods will not only naturally reduce inflammation but also give you a total sense of well-being.

Ultimately, what you place on your plate will help you control inflammation. Quercetin, fatty acids,

Omega 3, Capsacain, Gingerols, Bromelain, and Curcumin, are essential elements that you need to aid in your war. These can be used in herbs, chili peppers, ginger, and turmeric.

Here are fantastic foods that help you naturally reduce the risk of inflammation:

- The fruits of Quercetin, such as apples and cerises, are high and thus help lower inflammation.
- Vegetables like broccoli, chocolate, coliflor, and kale can help reduce inflammation considerably and naturally.
- The evil breath duo, Onions and Garlic, are two of the best foods for all types of pain. A large number of diseases that plague the human body can be cured or relieved. We have absolutely magnificent healing properties, and Quercetin is again very healthy.

- Bromelain-rich pineapples are perfect for pain relief. We help maintain pain and swelling.
- Omega-3 oils, found in oily fish like herring, sardines, salmon, and mackerel, work great, and naturally, combat inflammation.

So if you are inflamed and do not want to use medicine prescribed by doctors, learn to reduce inflammation by using these products to counter inflammation naturally.

Fruits, spices, vegetables, nuts, and fish are just some foods for inflammation reduction. Find out how these foods could help your body combat inflammation and why your daily diet needs them.

Here is some essential news for those who continuously suffer from inflammatory pain and discomfort-there are foods that can actually help.

If these foods are included in your everyday diet, you will get natural nutrients and chemicals to prevent inflammation. What foods will help you fight this problem? What are some?

Essential nutrients to fight inflammation: You want a diet that is rich in vitamin A, calcium, vitamin B, and omega-3 fatty acids to reduce pain, discomfort, and swelling due to inflammation.

The anti-inflammatory diet includes foods that not only suppress inflammation but also provide nutrients necessary to make the body function properly and healthily.

Here is a necessary means of combating inflammation by following the right anti-inflammatory diet.

Enjoy fruits and vegetables in abundance.

Make sure you eat plenty of fruit like bananas, strawberries, pineapples, cherries, and vegetables; like broccoli, chocolate, and spinach. Both products are fiber-rich and naturally anti-inflammatory. Some of the plants, fruits, and herbs contain polyphenols and bioflavonoids, which can also help combat free radicals that damage the body.

Eat large quantities of seafood.

Fish and their oils, in particular, are rich sources of omega-three fatty acids. Omega 3, in turn, contains DHA, and EPA fatty acids are protein and hormone building blocks that help fight inflammation. Omega 3 fish oil-rich foods include sardines, tuna, salmon, and halibut.

Make sure you have ample essential fatty acids in your diet.

You'll have to eat lots of fish if you want to enjoy the anti-inflammatory effects of fish oils.

Given the risk of mercury contamination and toxicity, it is safer to use omega-3 fish oil supplements in essential fatty acids. Fish oil supplements have been refined and checked to ensure they are safe and effective to produce anti-inflammatory effects.

Hold other things secret.

If certain foods reduce inflammation, there are foods that can increase inflammation. Ensure allergens and dietary irritants such as milk, eggs, gluten, and nuts are not avoided. It will help you to find time to identify and prevent your sensitivities.

Obtain natural relief from inflammation. A natural approach to cure your body of inflammation is taking food to reduce inflammation, without prescription medicine. As you know, NSAIDs and steroids may cause serious side effects, including heart and gastrointestinal problems. medication for inflammation

Ask your doctor about diet and the best ways to help you relieve pain and discomfort when you suffer from inflammation. Make sure you eat the right type of food to reduce inflammation and avoid those that increase inflammation, most likely.

Such claims are not medical advice nor have the Food and Drug Administration reviewed them.

Supplements shall not be formulated for diagnosis, rehabilitation, cure, care, or disease prevention.

Fighting INFLAMMATION, A Bite at the Time

Several things contribute to sedentary lifestyles, overweight, smoking, increased stress and lack of sleep, etc. Such factors and our US Standard Diet lead to low inflammatory rates that speed up the aging process and increase your risk of disease.

Because inflammation is a factor in promoting disease, measures to neutralize the inflammatory process are essential. Luckily, nature has created a lot to help us combat inflammation. Some foods have anti-inflammatory characteristics that can reduce inflammatory discomfort. The introduction into your current diet of foods that fight inflammation will improve your health and allow you to feel better. A natural inflammation strategy will reduce the dependence on prescription drugs and help to reduce their side effects.

First of all, however, let us look at foods that cause inflammation. Foods fried or made with hydrogenated vegetable oils are a significant contributor to inflammation. Ingredients are high in sugar too. This includes white sugar, cakes, white meal, cookies, fried food, and potato chips. Reducing the intake of sugar will reduce inflammation and help you cut calories to aid with weight loss and lower joint pain. Inflammation can worsen most processed foods, red meat, high sugar and processed carbohydrates.

Saturated fats also cause inflammation. Reduce your saturated fat intake by selecting lean meat cuts, cutting excess fat, and selecting low-fat milk products. Red meat arachidonic acid transforms into pro-inflammatory compounds. Healed meats like bacon have nitrates that enhance the inflammatory process. Another way to reduce the intake of saturated fat is to minimize the use of red meat.

Another issue in the inflammatory process is overweight. Fat cells make inflammatory body chemicals. See that your calorie intake is even addressed by anti-inflammatory foods.

Now, foods that battle inflammation to eat!

Antioxidants contribute to reducing inflammation by trapping free radicals. Fruits and Vegetables are good sources of dietary antioxidants. There is no limit to the positive benefit of eating fruit and vegetables for your body. Eating a variety of vegetables and fruits offers your body various antioxidants that can reduce inflammation together. The brighter the fruit and vegetables, the higher the antioxidant content, the general rule. It will also increase your fiber intake by eating more fruit and vegetables. People who consume more food are less inflamed.

- Pineapple is the right choice because it contains Bromelain, a protein-breaking enzyme. For many people, the effect of over the counter pain medications such as NSAIDs (for example, aspirin and ibuprofen) is similar in pain relief. Don't try to take Bromelain substitute. Please note that Bromelain thins the blood, so consult with your doctor if you are on a prescription blood thinner.

- Profit from vibrant beers like strawberries, blueberries, blackberries, pigmeat, raspberries, and red grapes. Use them in stevia-sweetened smoothies and desserts. Anti-oxidants are also contained in the cherries. Berry and cherry are high in fiber and low in fat and are an excellent substitute for white processed sugar for their natural sweetness. Cherries are also helpful for people with gout, as the body can wash uric acid that is crystallized to cause pain.

- Pomegranate were also shown to promote inflammation. Pomegranate extract led to decreased chemical development, causing inflammation. The dose used in the study is equivalent to drinking about 6 ounces of pomegranate juice a day.

Another significant nutrient source that prevents the inflammatory process is vegetables. Most plants have high carotenoid concentrations, another antioxidant. These also have calcium and VITAMIN C concentrations.

- Onion and garlic. These are large bulbs of Quercetin, a compound that serves as a natural antihistamine. Garlic also helps stimulate the fight against disease in your immune system. There are many other fruits and vegetables, including quercetin, black and green tea, capers, bananas, cherries, citrus fruit, onions, broccoli, raspberries, and the cactus fruit.

- Spinach is also high in carotenoids, and vitamin E. chard, kale, turnip greens, and mustard greens can also give you similar benefits.

- Sweet pats are sweet, low-calorie, fat-free, health-enhancing minerals and provide more carotenoids to combat inflammation. All the colorful vegetables, such as carrots, winter squash, red peppers, which have a high carotenoid content.

- Broccoli has high levels of calcium and vitamin C and also prevents inflammation of the skin. Steam your broccoli gently to take advantage of its safety.

Several spices are useful to combat inflammation. These include garlic, ginger, and peppers of hot chili. You can take the above spices in capsule form, but experimenting with them in different recipes is fun. The function of these spices is similar to anti-inflammatory pharmaceutical products but easier on the stomach.

- Turmeric or curcumin has been used in Asian medicine for chronic pain and stomach discomfort for a long time. Blood sugar, blood pressure, and cholesterol can also be reduced.

- Ginger has similar advantages to turmeric for reducing inflammation, and arthritis pain has also shown some ease. Ginger can also assist with car disease.

- Alternatively, oregano, parsley, thyme, basil, cinnamon, rosemary can also be used to reduce inflammation. Use a selection of toxic spices to take advantage of all health benefits.

Omega 3 fatty acids are among the best fighters we could use for inflammation. It can stimulate the immune system and fight inflammation by eating several servings of fish a week like cod, sardines, mackerel, tuna, and lobster. Among black, vegetables, green walnuts, and almonds, Omega 3's can also be found. Coconut and flaxseed oil are also excellent sources of fatty acids from omega 3.

Omega-3s play their part in reducing chronic inflammatory body changes and can make the pain of diseases such as arthritis more severe. These can also increase the risk of heart disease if they are taken regularly. You should take a fish oil supplement to harvest these health benefits if you don't like fish. Fish oil dilutes the blood, too. Please advise your doctor before any surgery to take fish oil or contact your doctor if you are in a coumadin or aspirin treatment before starting fish oil.

Other oils useful for reducing inflammation include:

- Olive Oil contains a natural oleocanthal compound that activates the same enzymes as approved anti-inflammatory drugs. Extra virgin olive oil contains just high enough of this chemical to be helpful.
- Omega 3 fatty acids are also found in Hemp Oil to reduce inflammation. This is a flexible oil that can either be cooked or taken with a tea cubicle.

Nuts are another excellent nutritional source to reduce inflammation.

- Walnuts contain vitamin E, which helps the immune system and can be eaten by handfuls or added to the dishes. These are also high in fatty acids of Omega 3.

Populations with the highest choline and betaine levels have a lower C-reactive protein, interleukin-6, and tumor necrosis factor. These are all inflammatory steps in the body. In your diet, chicken liver, eggs, beef liver, wheat germ, and dried soybeans are a good part of choline-rich foods. The foods rich in Betaine include wheat bran, spinach, lettuce, shrimp, and wheat bread.

Begin with some anti-inflammatory foods or dietary supplements. You'll help the cardiovascular system tremendously, and that exercise soreness. Acne, sinusitis, and painful joints may decrease. You may also reduce waist size due to lower calorie consumption.

Controlling Inflammation And Pain

Most of us now know that it is important to eat fish and to take our fish oils to preserve our memory and lubricate our joints. What are we doing, though, when our body starts to seize, our bones and cramps are painful, and we have arthritis?

Inflammation is often the direct cause of arthritis joint pain and tissue damage. The choice of foods to reduce inflammation is essential, such as the avoidance of refined, processed, and manufactured foods, as they contain inflammatory fats, preservatives, and carbohydrates.

Inflammation of Omega 6 fatty acids can be increased. They are found in soybean oil, often used in cookies and snacks. The maize syrup that is commonly used as a sweetener is another concern. It is a carbohydrate that we digest rapidly, but that disturbs the metabolism that, in some instances, causes inflammation.

Extra virgin olive oil, contains the antioxidant (polyphenol) to help protect tissues against inflammation. Omega 3 (oily fish like salmon, sardines, and herring) can help reduce inflammation. Inflammation. We must eat fish three days a week, but as we all know, the supplements of fish oil are essential for arthritis patients.

Better carbohydrates must also be differentiated from the poor by recognizing the glycemic index and their effect on blood sugar. Blood glucose management reduces inflammation so that low-type foods such as whole grains, sweet potatoes, beans, and squash substitute high glycemic foods made with sugar and flour. If you have pasta to eat, but not too often. It's better than fruit and eggs. You also need less protein from animals, especially red meat and chicken, as these contain a potentially inflammatory amino acid. Use more vegetable protein like beans and soy, instead. It is also essential to check if you have sensitivities in wheat and yeast because these will make all your cells in your body even more responsive.

Outside of your list, fruit and vegetables are a must. Choose three colors per day and add ginger and turmeric, both with anti-inflammatory effects. An excellent anti-inflammatory drink is also made from green tea.

Celery is vital for arthritis because it has anti-inflammatory and anti-rheumatic properties in the list of supplements. This detoxify helps the kidneys dispose of waste and is perfect for digestion. It is useful for rheumatism and gout with bioflavonoids.

Hydrochloride glucosamine is another addition that can regenerate cartilage and synovial fluid. It is critical that you take it every day and two capsules a day at the same time. After about 3-6 weeks, you won't see the results and don't take them if you are allergic to fish. Sometimes the stomach gets very irritated and loose bowel movements, but this occurs only in a few individuals. You just have to tell your doctor if you are a diabetic or if you are taking other drugs temporarily.

Glucosamine sulphate, a natural component of our glucose-formed bodies, is another member of the glucosamine group. Cartilage and synovial fluid that helps the joints to coat are essential. As we enhance our ability to make this decrease, in some cases, osteoarthritis has been stopped. It can be used as a preventive measure. Osteoarthritis is right for the knee and sometimes stronger than ibuprofen. It contributes to reducing the risk of training injuries to athletes and sportspeople. Patients with arthritis should take 1500 mg for acute pain and 500-1000 mg for general maintenance. It doesn't work as quickly as drugs and should be considered for at least six weeks.

Because everyone is different if you are not sufficient, seek Devils Claw, another herbal remedy to relieve inflammation and pain. Start taking 1-2 ml three times a day of the tincture.

If you have successfully treated homeopathic remedies, try Bryonia that can help with rheumatism and arthritis, chest problems, and headaches. Get it from a homeopath. It often helps for swollen, painful rheumatic joints.

If you want something else on the tea line, consider Cats Claw, a wooden wine grown in Peru's rainforests. The Indians traditionally used it for the diagnosis of arthritis. It has immune-stimulating activity, anti-viral, antioxidant, anti-inflammatory effects, anti-tumor, and anti-microbial effects. It is also available in capsules.

Always note that your digestion is important because it is essential to have proper digestion to consume nutrients and your food. Otherwise, you will load up with pills, and they will just move through you with hardly any beneficial effects. Ginger is moist, perfect for digestion, circulation, prevents inflammation, and reduces blood pressure. It also leads to pain relief. Study shows it to be as effective as anti-inflammatory non-steroidal medications in Copenhagen but without its side effects. It is, however, slower to function and takes approximately three weeks to alleviate symptoms. A successful preventive or long-term ailment is 500 mg daily.

In addition to the above, 12 biochemical tissue salts contribute to the health of the body. Ferr Phos (iron phosphate) is used for acute fever attacks, swollen, and bruised joints, and sore joints when exacerbated by motion. When conditions are of acidity, Nat Phos (sodium phosphate) is useful and alternates Nat Sulph (sodium chloride-ordinary salt) to Nat Mur when joint creaks, Mag Phos (magnesium phosphate) alternating with Calc Phos (calcium phosphate) for the pain relief of osteoarthritis. It is sometimes helpful to mix Ferr Phos, Nat Phos, Nat Sulph, and Silica, which was a treatment called Zief, which was painful in 1964. The chewable, biochemical salts are essential as these are usually more effective.

The above is a long list and can not emphasize enough that different things work very well for different people, but arthritis can be controlled with the right diet, and your system can be alkalized and proper supplements. Consult a healthy health plan with your natural practitioner. It is necessary not to' self-medicate' so far, and it is not enough to have a 10-minute conversation with a doctor in a health food store. You need proper, thorough evaluation by a Naturopath or Nutritionist who wants to clearly meet your needs and take other diseases and symptoms into account too.

CHAPTER THREE

The Glossopharyngeal Nerve and Vagus Nerve and Their Disorders

As these two cranial nerves are closely linked, they are described here — the sensory and motor parts of the glossopharyngeal nerve. The motor fibers come from the vague nucleus in the side of the medulla. They leave the skull with their vagus and accessory nerves through the jugular foramen. They provide the stylopharyngeal muscle, which raises the pharynx.

Autonomous efferent nerve fibers are produced from the lower salivatory nucleus. Preganglionic fibers travel through the less superficial petrosal nerve to the otic ganglion, and postganglionic fibers travel through the fifth nerve aural-temporal branch to the Parotid gland. The nucleus of the glossopharyngeal nerve sensory fibers are found in the petrous ganglion below the jugular foramen and also in the tiny superior ganglion. The external threads provide for facial tonsils, back walls of the pharynx, part of the soft palate, and taste sensations from the back of the tongue.

The vagus is the longest of all the cranial nerves. The engine fibers, with the exception of tensor veli palate and stylopharyngeus, come from the nucleus ambiguous and supply all pharynx, soft palate, and larynx muscles. The parasympathetic fibers originate from the dorsal efferent nucleus and leave the medulla for the craniosacral part of the autonomous nervous system as preganglionic fibers.

Such fibers end up in the ganglia near the viscera, supplied by post-ganglion fibers. The role is parasympathetic. This produces bradycardia, bronchial constriction, gastric and pancreatic juice secretions, and increased peristalsis. The sensory component of the vagus has its nuclei in the jugular nodosum ganglion. The vagus has sensations of the backside of the external auditory meat and neighboring pinna and pain sensation of the dura mater on the back of the cranial fossa.

Testing: Testing the 9th and 10th nerve functions together are better, as they are usually jointly affected. Inquire for signs such as dysphagia, dysarthria, nasal fluid regurgitation, and speech rush. The engine part is tested by checking the uvula when the patient is opened. The Uvula is usually in the middle. The palatal arch is flattened and diminished ipsilaterally in unilateral vagal paralysis. The uvula has deviated to the good side during phonation.

A stimulus such as a cotton or tongue blade in the posterior pharyngeal or tonsilar wall is used to stimulate the reflex or pharyngeal reflex. If the reflection is present, the pharyngeal musculature may increase and contract, followed by retraction of the tongue. The afferent arc of this reflex is protected by the vagus, while the efferent one is by the glossopharyngeal. This reflection is lost in either ninth or tenth lesions of the nerve. Test for general sensations on the back of the pharyngeal wall, soft palate, facial tonsils, and taste for the rear third tongue. In glossopharyngeal paralysis, these are affected.

Isolated involvement of the ninth and tenth nerve is rare and is usually involved together, often affecting the eleventh and twelfth nerve. Glossopharyngeal neuralgia is much less common but similar to trigeminal neuralgia. There is severe paroxysmal pain in the throat of the tonsillar fossa. It may be related to bradycardia and is called vago glossopharyngeal neuralgia in these cases.

A phenytoin or carbamazepine trial usually works to relieve pain. Brain lesions such as motor neuron disease, lateral medulla infarction, and Bulbar poliomyelitis may jointly affect these nerves and cause bulbar paralysis. These nerves outside the brain stem may be affected by post-fossa tumors and basal meningitis. Total vagal bilateral disease is life incompatible. The recurrent laryngeal nerves in thoracic lesions, especially on the left, cause only a voice heartbeat without dysphagia.

Chronic Depression is As Terrible As Any Disease

Chronic depression is also known as dysthymic disorder. The condition may be extreme but not as severe as major depression. Someone you know may have, and you wouldn't say chronic depression. A healthy life for people with this condition is very likely. It is not unusual for them to continue daily activities such as going to school or having a social life without significant problems. Of course, the outside world is invisible because the symptoms of this illness are on the inside. The results are both physical and mental.

It also noticed that if the family member had become chronically depressed by the age of 13, the relatives surveyed were six times more likely to have chronic depression.

Researchers don't know what causes dysthymia. A type of chronic depression is suspected to be associated with brain changes involving serotonin, a chemical or neurotransmitter that helps the brain cope with emotions. Significant life stressors, chronic diseases, medicines, and relationships or work problems may also increase the likelihood of dysthymia.

A professional in mental health usually makes the diagnosis based on the symptoms of the person. In the event of dysthymia, the symptoms will have lasted longer than those with severe depression and will be less severe. Medication psychotherapy is usually the best possible treatment option for almost everybody for depression (chronic or acute). If you just do one, you probably won't get well as fast, and it's that simple. We have decades of research that prove this, but here's another to add to the list.

Chronic depression won't make you cough, sneeze, or fever. Typically there won't be a rash. However, a victim of this disease can suffer from impotence, insignificance, and desperate feelings. Some people with chronic depression sometimes give up their treatment on one or the other modality.

Despite years of therapy, for example, you will surely feel that it is pointless if you have not felt less discouraged. The same goes for years if you use the same antidepressant and find that it helps only a little. Many affected can experience sleep and insomnia problems. The patient may be consumed by constant feelings of sadness and vacuum.

Neither psychotherapy alone nor medication alone differed significantly in terms of their efficacy in aiding a person with depression in this study–the two were equally effective. However, the researchers found that neither treatment alone was as efficient as the combination of the two. Many people with chronic depression often give up on one side or the other. Despite years of therapy, for example, you may undoubtedly feel that it is of little use if you have not felt less depressed. The same goes for years when you are taking the same medication, and yet it only seems to be a little beneficial.

Death and suicide are factors for a patient. People with chronic depression usually hide these symptoms well. One will look very carefully for signs and symptoms when mental illness occurs. We are not always clear. They are not still clear. What are the dysthymia signs and symptoms?

The symptoms of dysthymia are similar but not as severe to those of major depression and include:

- Persistent sleeping (too much or too little)
- Feels of helplessness, hopelessness, and worthlessness
- Feelings of shame
- Loss of interest or self-pleasure
- Energy loss or tiredness
- Insomnia (early morning awakening)
- Difficulties to focus, to think or to decide

- Changing appetite (over-crowding or loss of appetite)

If you have the signs of depression for more than two weeks, a psychiatrist or a doctor is necessary to consult. The physician carries out an extensive medical examination with particular attention to the clinical history of both your family and your own.

Several laboratory tests, such as X-rays or blood tests for dysthymia, are carried out.

A mental health specialist typically treats chronic depression based on the individual's symptoms. Dysthymia usually leads to less severe symptoms of depression and lasts longer than people with severe depression.

Studies have shown that a complex system of brain neurotransmitters generates chemicals, which transmit signals between nerve cells, depending on the activity of the brain. One of these neurotransmitters, serotonin, creates a sense of gladness or well-being. Medicines used to remedy neurotransmitter imbalances are very effective in treating depression. This is why depression is believed to be caused as a result of chemical imbalances in the brain. And with respect to heredity, depression has often arisen in families.

The doctor will want to ensure that your symptoms do not result from substance abuse or a medical condition like hypothyroidism or dysthymia. Depression and other manifestations in psychological, educational, or other areas of your life should also cause clinically significant depression or disability.

'Depression is the fourth most impaired disease in the world, but we don't know anything about what it does or how it progresses in the brain,' he says. Potash states that the condition is one of the most important public health issues. Psychotherapeutic therapy allows the psychiatrist to try to identify the cause of depression and to establish a positive perspective for the patient. The other way to help manage the condition is to prescribe antidepressants. In many cases, both methods are used to produce a positive outcome. Note, parents who were never stressed were not included in the report. The chances cited, therefore, do not extend to the whole population.

Although chronic depression is not major depression, it can certainly lead to that depression. Early detection is essential. Although chronic depression is a severe condition, it can be treated. Dysthymia is usually treated with a combination of psychotherapy and medicine. Medicines help to remedy chemical imbalances and to relieve depression symptoms.

Psychotherapy helps solve personal problems that could lead to depression. Around 14 million Americans have chronic, mentally, and socially handicapped depression. These people are often misdiagnosed with disturbances of character and personality.

Chronic depression typically becomes an issue when the illness starts to cause problems in everyday life. It is time to act when jobs or other external activities begin to suffer.

While dysthymia is a severe disease, it is also highly treatable. Early diagnosis and health treatment can, as with any chronic illness, reduce the intensity and time of depression symptoms and also reduce the chance of a recurrence.

Doctors can use psychotherapy (counseling), antidepressants, or a combination of these treatments to treat dysthymia. Dysthymia is often treatable solely with the help of primary care physicians.

Most people with chronic depression are not looking for treatment because they don't want to accept they have a mental health condition. Nevertheless, people with chronic depression can lead healthy, productive lives with proper treatment. See a doctor if you have chronic depression. The person can assist you in building a treatment plan to feel the way you want it. They are taking the recommended dose at about the same time every day if your doctor prescribes an antidepressant.

Don't stop taking your medication or skip a dose without your doctor's approval, even if you feel great. Antidepressants must be gradually reduced in order to prevent side effects. It is also essential to work with a therapist or a support group to help with any of your depression issues. You will develop a positive attitude and a new way of looking at your life and problems.

Recognizing and monitoring your symptoms is an essential step in your recovery. And don't forget that what you eat, how much sleep you get, and how much exercise you all make, makes you feel good. If you or someone you know has suicidal ideas, call your doctor or therapist straight away. Also, call your doctor if your antidepressant has any adverse side effects.

It's not time that people suffering from chronic depression have a straight jacket. They have issues that must be addressed and carefully and supportively addressed. Everyone is vulnerable to the risk of this disease. Learning that can support or benefit a loved one in the future.

What Is a Chronic Illness?

Chronic illness or chronic disease is a long-term medical condition that persists or continues. Although genetics and heredity can be related to certain chronic diseases, those are acquired from the environment and the most common lifestyle. Aging also plays an essential role in the progression of a chronic illness or disorder, as people are more vulnerable to this type of disease when the body gets older.

For example, elderly people are prone to cancer, even while maintaining a healthy lifestyle. They are consuming alcohol, smoking, using illegal substances, increasing the risk of contracting chronic diseases, and increasing the body's harm.

Some of this chronic illness includes high blood pressure or hypertension, asthma, and cancer. Although most of these diseases cannot be healed, medicine can regulate them. With technological advances, especially in medicine, there are now more ways to tackle chronic diseases. Several drugs have been found to control these diseases, and some even help cure them.

It is essential to be well aware of chronic diseases so that they can be appropriately treated. It is like shooting a bunch of rockets at a mosquito without having the necessary information or permission from the physician or a professional. It could not lead to a solution and occasionally cause even more problems.

A good understanding of how chronic condition functions can be a significant weapon in its prevention. Cancer, for example, has many forms, and it can be treated by checking, and laboratory testing growing cancer has infected the body.

Chronic illness or chronic diseases require extensive treatment. This affects not only the physical body but also the mental and emotional wellbeing. Many people with chronic conditions may need care and therapy to boost their overall progress.

A patient with a chronic disease will need all the help they can get, and while regular medication can help alleviate pain, family, and friends, support is as vital as these drugs. As straightforward as it may sound, nobody knows when death will come, and people with chronic conditions are becoming more overwhelming in their thinking. The social support can help them cope with this reality even better than chronic diseases alone.

A healthy diet and ethical practices are the two main factors that decrease the risk of these diseases and should be followed on a regular basis. A trip to the doctor's office and proper physical examination would also help prevent chronic diseases. There are many facilities in South Africa that offer medical assistance, especially for people with chronic conditions — educating them in chronic disease care and prevention.

Prevention is better than cure, and prevention is best before it is too late at an early stage.

PILLARS OF CHRONIC ILLNESS

For all the attention paid in the past few decades to health, exercise and nutrition, diets, and the "miracles of medicine," our organization is seeing a drastic increase in all chronic diseases. These include cancer, cardiovascular disease, obesity, diabetes, depression and anxiety disorders, osteoarthritis, Alzheimer's and dementia, acid reflux, autoimmune problems, constipation, infertility, chronic fatigue, chronic pain, reduced drive and more.

Science continues to show that over 99 percent of these diseases are genuinely avoidable— they are not "genetic," as the message has been maintained so long. Our lifestyle choices and climate decide whether we communicate health and well-being or not. The science of epigenetics sums up this relationship between the environment and our genetic expression.

There are obviously some causal associations established in chronic disease analysis. We do not develop chronic diseases due to random chance or genetic defects. The constant disease foundations are the prerequisites for chronic disease. Without at least one of these five elements, we do not establish chronic disease.

Pillars of Chronic Illness:

- Stress Hormones
- Insulin resisting
- Chronic inflammation

- Reducing SHBG (sex hormone globulin binding)
- Diminished immunity

For instance, discovering someone who had at least one of the pillars first would be doubtful, many would say impossible. In the most straightforward metaphors, cancer, or any of the other chronic diseases could be associated with cooked potato. The potato didn't end that way naturally. The spud was not made by bad luck or lousy potato genes. Something must have followed the end result of the cooking of that potato.

It was baked, roasted, slowly cooked, fried, microwaved. Or any of these variations. Such forms of cooking are like the five pillars. You will precede a potato fried! For example, chronic disease development is much more complicated and thorough than food. But if we don't grasp the structure of how illness actually occurs, we can never recover health in its entirety.

The five elements are necessarily intelligent physiological adaptation to a different level of precursors in the case of chronic diseases. For the organism to respond in the form of these pillars or adjustments to the environment, toxicity and deficiency must predominate.

It ensures that lifestyle choices are made that do not adhere to our genetic health program and chronic disease prevention. Whether the option of the lifestyle is linked to diet, activity, or attitude-if toxic and weak, rather than pure and enough, the body will intelligently communicate adaptations in the form of physiological stress responses to this toxic and deficient environment. The five pillars of chronic disease clearly outline this response.

The reaction to physiological stress does not contribute to health; it does not cure. This allows for short-term survival in the pathogenic environment. In essence, it takes time to get to a healthy environment-less toxic and deficient, purer, and more adequate.

The unhealthy and ineffective habits are like a rock on the backpack we carry as we tread water. When the stones are left behind, and more foundations are selected, our bodies take the knowledgeable decision to adapt to this new environment.

The body tries to maintain equilibrium in a changing environment. This is referred to as allostasis. The rocks are known as the allostatic load-the cumulative effect of our body on stressors (toxicity and shortcomings).

The physiological stress response and five pillars of chronic disease are caused by this allostatic load. We don't pass to the next stage without the rocks.

If therefore, we can avoid putting the rock in our backpack first of all (by making clear and sufficient lifestyle choices consistently) and remove the stone that is already there (by reducing toxic and deficient decisions), then our organism has no more reason to express these five pillars. They do not develop chronic diseases without any of the five components.

The key to this relationship between chronic disease and the environment is our lifestyle choices.

Preventing Chronic Illness By Healthy Eating

Healthy eating can significantly lower the likelihood that chronic diseases such as heart disease, stroke, high blood pressure, and diabetes will develop. Preventing illness by proper nutrition is only one of the advantages of healthy eating.

The incidence of heart disease is probably and most likely risk of a poor diet. Foods with high levels of saturated fats, cholesterol, sugar, and sodium contribute to weight gain and increase the risk of heart disease. Proper nutrition has benefits such as decreasing bad cholesterol, increasing good cholesterol, lowering blood pressure, and regulating body weight. By reducing your diet's fat, reducing your salt intake, reducing sugar, eating lots of fruit and vegetables You will reduce your chances of developing heart disease considerably.

For chronic diseases that evolve from poor eating habits, diabetes comes a close second to heart disease. Many of the same factors that cause heart disease also contribute to diabetes growth. Healthy eating is one of the critical steps in avoiding the onset of diabetes. Supported foods should be consumed daily, such as whole grains and fresh vegetable items. Overweight makes you more likely to develop diabetes. A 5-10% weight loss of your body weight will reduce the risk of diabetes by 60%. You dramatically increase the chances of overweight and diabetes by choosing to eat unhealthy foods. The good news is that dietary changes can quickly reduce these risks.

Too often, people do not know that poor nutrition can lead to cancer growth. Cancer is the second leading cause of death for Americans. They also believe that cancer is just the misfortune of drawing. Genetics may play a part in this, but chance doesn't have anything to do with cancer. Scientists show that the leading cause of the disease is a lifestyle choice. Smoking through tobacco and excess stress, sun exposure, and poor nutrition are only a few factors linked to cancer growth.

The chapter focuses on proper nutrition in relation to health problems and thus, on the cause. Researchers have found that red meat can be associated with almost one-third of all cancers. Researchers have also found a connection between sugar and the growth of certain diseases. Charred foods are yet another possible cause of cancer. Alcohol consumption also increases the risk of cancer.

A poor diet will increase the risk of many other diseases. Improving your diet will substantially reduce the risk of life-threatening conditions. Taking these improvements will also improve your overall health and make you feel better.

PREVENTING CHRONIC ILLNESS BY GETTING PHYSICAL ACTIVITY WHEN SITTING

A short summary of preventing chronic disease percentage of deaths associated with inadequate physical activity that adults regularly engage in at least 150 minutes of medium intensity aerobic physical activity equivalent.

Inadequate rates of physical activity were due to a significant share of deaths. Increasing the level of physical activity of adults to comply with the current guidelines may be one way to minimize the risk of premature death, smoking is new.

One of my most profound experiences was about ten years ago when a man was in a coma sitting in a hospital room. He walked out during angioplasty and opened the heart's arteries and lay in a coma a few months later. The man, although an intelligent man, a queen's counsel in many ways, thought our belief in a proper diet and exercise was "discharge." While in a coma, every hour, physical therapists came to work for him not only to stop bed rash but also to work on pumping his muscles. That is only necessary.

Most North Americans sit an average of 13 hours a day and sleep for an average of 8 hours, leading to a sedentary lifestyle of around 21 hours a day.

Have you got a desk job, spend a lot of time commuting, outside the TV, computer and dining table? Experts say that we should get up at work at least two hours a day for those who have a desk job, and strive for four.

There is a wide range of training equipment for the workstation. Take a look at the best prices. A significant investment in your health, your money, your concentration, and your productivity! An excellent investment for employers, workstations offer workers satisfaction, safety, and productivity (brain oxygenation), and gratitude.

Another significant investment is a heart monitor or a wearable device that monitors at a minimum activity and heart rate. Do not think the calories burned out in most apps. Finally, we want to increase the prices of movement and use the precious weight of the muscle.

Use it

- Keep your desk resistance bands.
- Who cares if someone's watching
- Tennis ball squeeze
- Raising your arm in the air and pushing, Pushing between knees.
- Ground feet: drive in place deep into the ground
- Push arms, push legs, torso twist.
- Great time to perform Kegel exercises-improve your urinary and sexual life. "Not turkey neck" exercises-always go to a chair
- Extend the neck gently, slowly, relieve stress and breathe deeply

- Get up and go three minutes an hour

- Drink the water which is so essential to your health and make you go to the toilet more often

- Hold a Wheel of Pilate at the desk-push a static force, such as the floor and the backbone.

- Isometric contractions

- Push hands against each other Not approved for high blood pressure patients.

- Most telephone calls can be made while standing. An infinite list is available.

And when you watch TV?

Don't just watch DWTS, Stars Dance. Don't just lie on a couch, do leg lifts, bridges. Core work chooses your favorite television series-and to do that from your sofa.

Life Combo: Our heart rate rises to pump additional nourishment and oxygen into these magnificent muscles. Respiratory speeds to get more oxygen and get more carbon dioxide rid. The more we work with muscles, the better the physical activity.

Aerobic activity to improve brain blood flow. Aerobic exercise can enhance our cardiovascular function and increase blood flow to the brain as well. It is also instrumental in oxygenating the body that improves the health of cells and tissue connections in your brain, and the BTW here, if you think you do not have any resources, no time, no strength or too sore—it is quite possible that you will not have adequate physical activity. The more you do physical activity, the more you want it.

Chronic Illness is a Disability

Disability is described by the Social Security Administration as the incapacity to participate in substantial gainful activities due to mental or physical impairments that are medically determinable and are likely to lead to death lasted or is expected to last no more than 12 months. While it appears that the definition would cover many disabilities, many disabled people feel that this definition of the disability does not cover them because of chronic disease. We are quick to point out that in most dictionaries, the concept of disability is "the state of failure to perform as a result of physical and mental disability."

The biggest problem with chronically disabled people seems to be the concept of disability in the Social Security Administration that is to take care of people with a' statics' invalidity, such as mental retardation, learning disabilities, blindness and some with many disabilities, like being a quadriplegic. Those with chronic disease are impaired, but they are not stagnant. Most days, they can function, while others can't, and when they are well or ill, there can't be predicted. Chronic disease is a condition that often prohibits you from living, doing normal everyday activities, and socializing, although it is not permanent or unchanging.

This' still evolving' type of disability presents system problems. Once a person receives disability benefits, he or she cannot work. When they decide to try to complete their nine-month job trial period and then keep doing' substantial productive jobs,' they lose their benefits. This is not cut and dry for those with chronic diseases. You can work comfortably for months or years only to suffer symptoms of your illness and be cared for weeks. While it takes 36 months for them to obtain benefits, they can come and go for three years, leaving them without any advantages after the extension period.

The program has no specific guidelines for those with continually changing chronic diseases. The most energetic people with a chronic illness will apply for benefits rather than jobs, and this leaves them with very little money. This will potentially change in the future.

CHAPTER FOUR

Living in Chronic Disease

To live with a chronic disease will mean changing the way of life before your diagnosis, at all levels, in physical, emotional, and psychological terms. If your condition is severe, even before you are diagnosed, you can worry about things you didn't even know about. If you deal with chronic diseases, you sometimes find that the simplest of things are now the most important things for you. You're angry, worried, irritated, tired, unhappy, nervous, and most likely lonely and tearful.

If you feel like this, it is always best to talk with a doctor or a psychologist or attach you to a knowledge and assistance group of fellow patients. Chronic illness therapy at a time like this can be beneficial.

Having assistance and support gives you greater confidence and makes you relax and cope better. It ensures that you have hope and opportunities for a positive result. The pain, sorrow, and rigidity that is often so constant are what make people feel the most. Pain management will help, and a number of options are available for people with chronic conditions, whether by drugs or natural therapy, to gain comforts.

Unlike acute pain that, although it can be severe, persists and persists relatively quickly with a chronic condition. For instance, someone with a toothache may have agonized for a while, but it may also end in a few hours or days, but any movement with arthritis may carry a continuous experience of pain and rigidity. You can't walk very far often, and many people have difficulty sleeping. Suitable treatments and drugs must be found.

If you have constant distress and pain over a period of time, even if it is initially not so painful or more annoying, it is better to check with a doctor to exclude any chronic condition before it takes its full hold.

You can still take time to find ways to avoid contracting these long-term diseases, such as maintaining a healthy diet and exercising regularly. Definitely, prevention is better than cure. Laughter also has a lot of health benefits. Laughter helps the body strengthen the immune system, relieve stress, and maintain a positive mindset in times of adversity.

COPE WITH CHRONIC ILLNESS

Chronic disease does not appear like pneumonia or a broken leg, but you know that you will recover in a certain amount of time. Chronic illness means you have no certitude as to when you can improve; in fact, your disease can never go away. You are often in pain and tired when you have a chronic illness; it can affect your physical abilities or your physical appearance. You may not function, causing financial anxiety and stress. You may also be angry, wondering why it happened to you. And it doesn't just affect you, of course. Family members and friends are also affected and influenced by a loved one's continuing health changes.

In these conditions, it is easy to be isolated; changes to your body and your abilities will affect your positive self-image, making it difficult for you to communicate with others. Stress can grow, prolongation, which then leads to frustration, resentment, desperation, and sometimes even depression.

When you have a chronic disease, one of the first things you should do is seek help. Don't leave until you have already struggled with the consequences of your new health status. You should create a support network as soon as you feel less competent and powerless. Someone in your place will help in several ways. A trained psychologist or therapist may help you make strategies to regain a sense of control and develop a recovery plan to meet your needs. You can also judge whether depression exists and, therefore, if you need additional medications to help regulate your mood, other than those that treat your physical illness.

Support groups are also helpful in providing an atmosphere in which you can learn new ways to cope. You can share approaches that you have discovered with others so that you cannot only be proactive in your diseases but also become stronger and realize that you are not alone in your condition.

Top Tips for Control

- Consider the illness. It might sound defective, but if you strive to adapt, then you can recognize your loss (that's happier when you were physically and emotionally strong) and help you face the new challenges of your life.
- See you today, and all that entails—your appearance, your disability, your problems, and your weaknesses. Take pride in what you can do now.

- Take full control of your health and never ignore all the help you can get.

- Become a disease specialist. Find it, speak to other doctors, always go to your medical appointments, armed with questions.

- Let go of the "Why me?" mentality and don't look back. Once you have quit the past, you will solve the problems you are currently experiencing, such as how to continue exercising despite new leg weaknesses.

And remember, you are always "YOU;" your life should not be controlled by the disease.

Learning how to handle a chronic disease is difficult, but once you find a way to do so while still "your," it will give you the strength to regain a positive physical, emotional and spiritual perspective on life before your illness.

Primary Causes of Chronic Illness

The number of people with mysterious diseases such as chronic fatigue and fibromyalgia is increasing in Western society at an alarming rate. Instead of trying to find the root cause of the disease, most doctors simply treat the symptoms. The simple fact is that the emphasis is on recovery rather than disease prevention.

Chronic diseases and degenerative diseases are the main contributors. These are mediocre food, contamination, and stress. Let's look quickly at each one.

Food Most people in American society are malnourished even if they eat the prescribed calorie diet for the year 2000. That is because most of the American diet consists of processed foods. Such products are vitamin and mineral extracted and are made of little more than bulk to fill a human. Non-commercial farms grow on land that is nutrient-depleted. The plants are damaged and coated with pesticides in order to keep them alive. Factory farm animals are often fed maize because it is cheap and they will bulk them so that they are ready for the market more quickly. The side effect is that the poor diet jeopardizes the animals' immune system. Therefore, the animals are kept in close proximity and exposed to their own excrement. The animals are given large quantities of antibiotics until they are ready to be sold. Add preservatives and aromatic compounds to this, and you have a disease formula.

When we eat animal and plant products that lack the nutrients we need, our own species are affected. The immune system stops working correctly without sufficient supplies of the building blocks that the body needs. In some cases, it starts attacking its own cells, which believe they are foreign invaders. In other cases, the immune cells are weakened, and external threats are simply not known. Clinical evidence has indicated that some chronic fatigue is due to bacteria such as mycoplasma and viruses like Epstein-Barr. In today's society, cancer is rife. One hundred years ago, in children and young adults, cancer was almost unheard of, but it is becoming increasingly prevalent.

Toxicity Today, we live in a toxic climate. Fluoride, arsenic, and other heavy metals contaminate our drinking water. Washing products do not kill contaminants because these substances are absorbed into the plant's root system. We consume specific amounts of chemicals when people eat certified organic goods. Within conventionally grown animal flesh, growth hormones and antibiotics are present. Automotive and construction waste polluted air-breathing.

Plastic containers are released over time, and contaminants can be leached into foodstuffs. Damping from household cleaners can grow over time in the body of a person. Even pots and pans of aluminum can leach into food.

Stress Modern society's rapid place is taking its toll on the bodies of people. The trend today is to do more with less. Americans work longer hours, take fewer vacations, and cope with more pressures than ever before. This is added to the real threat of being laid off. The body has a cortisol-regulated fight or flight response built-in. In fact, our ancestors were threatened with their lives by their climate, so the fight or flight approach worked well. During sometimes brief blasts, high cortisol and adrenalin levels are not a concern. The problem in today's world is that the reaction never turns off, and the long-term effects are adverse.

The Perfect Storm Poor nutrition, toxicity, and stress create a perfect storm for chronic disease development. The above effects are cumulative. Nobody develops chronic fatigue or nighttime cancer. This occurs after years of poor eating habits, environmental exposure, and years of stress.

CHRONIC ILLNESS IS EPIDEMIC

The only threat to life in the US is not terrorism, oil scarcity, or political events. Chronic disease is now an epidemic in the US. On every front, illness is growing. For the very first time since Richard Nixon declared war on cancer in 1975, the disease will be the leading killer this year. One adult every 2.3 contacts a form of invasive cancer, most of them dying. Cancer is today the number one cause of death in children between the ages of three and fourteen. About 1/2 of all Americans now live in severe safety conditions. Sixty million more Americans live with a variety of chronic conditions. Examples of several chronic conditions include cancer, diabetes, arthritis, asthma, glaucoma, and cardiac disease. Tragically, most people are unaware of the threat. You have to protect your health, it is imperative, it threatens even your life.

The United States spends more money than any nation in the world on health care, yet it ranks among the sickest developed countries in the world. Further people than ever have been on prescription medication. The threat is so near home. Life goes on, but there's fear somewhere in the back of the mind. Minimal effort is made to educate the public on environmental issues, nutrition, and natural alternative prevention.

The EPA ranks toxic toxins 70 times indoors higher than outdoors. The risk of cancer in your own home is three times higher than in the outside world. Due to the seriousness of these statistics, what is difficult to understand is remarkably little. When something is said, facts are so surprising that it is difficult to believe it is true.

Over 70 chronic health problems are associated with free radicals present in the contaminated climate. Such chemicals can be found in food, water, and air. Free radicals invade cells and can kill entire DNA strands. There is very little research on why we get sick. Often work on the development of medication is carried out to treat symptoms when we are ill. There is very little research or training on disease prevention.

Knowledge is the most critical factor impacting health and well-being in the future. Almost all of us are unaware of the danger in and around us every day. In the industrialized world of the West, there are dominant players and enormous corporate profits. For instance, pharmaceutical companies have long learned that the treatment of symptoms with medicines is more beneficial than patient education and prevention.

Nothing is more precious than your wellbeing. It is, by far, the most precious commodity. There is no other more critical responsibility than protecting your health and the health of your family. You can do just that with the right science and clinically proven mix of nutrients.

It may be difficult to believe that nutrition is so powerful. That the right scientifically combined nutrients can, in many situations, do more for the body than a drug — the healing systems of our bodywork. You know how to cure. It's fantastic to see a cut close and often leave no scar. The body's internal healing mechanisms can be triggered by a natural combination of all vitamins, minerals, and antioxidants at optimal levels.

How Lifestyle Choices Are Causing to Sink Into Chronic Illness

The current science continues to show that our health and chronic illness are not our genes but our climate. More than 1% of chronic diseases are actually inherited in nature. In fact, this means that chronic illness can be avoided.

Nevertheless, the diagnosis of over 50% of the American population is Chronic Disease, and almost 80% of all healthcare expenditures (doctor's appointments, medications, hospitalization, etc.) are a result of these lifestyle disorders.

In the next few years, this number is expected to increase astronomically. Some claim that this single problem is going to bankrupt our country. This is especially interesting as science tells us that this is totally preventable!

What are the chronic conditions? The list includes cancer, heart disease, diabetes, obesity, depression, infertility, autoimmune conditions and disorders, Alzheimer's, dementia, chronic tiredness, insomnia, chronic pain, constipation, acid reflux, and decreased sex drive, etc.

With such a vast list, it is difficult to imagine how we can avoid such conditions first of all, from forming. They seem to be so unrelated. In order to understand our role in chronic disease prevention, we must first be able to understand simply how chronic disease develops in our environment.

To understand how our lifestyle and our climate are linked to chronic diseases, imagine that you fall into a pool of water as your life begins. You have two things to do: swelling water wings and an empty backpack.

Your wings were swollen for you, but they have a prolonged leak. It is predicted that their air will last for 120 years (the useful lifetime). When the air bursts, you have less time left. It's going to get older! If these water wings are not interfered with, they will last you 120 years all.

Whenever you choose a lifestyle that does not adhere to your inherent genetic health needs, you put a "tar" into your backpack. Our health plan and excellent work include cleanliness and sufficiency in our feeding, traveling, and thought. This means that we give our bodies exactly what is needed for optimal health (purity) and adequate (sufficiency).

Indeed, we consider unsafe and defective lifestyle choices in our strategy for excellent work. The toxicity and impairment of homeostatic cell function are inconsistent. Therefore, the rocks in your backpack become these poisonous and defective options.

These stones (stressors) can come from any lifestyle field: poor dietary choices, sedentary living, unhealthy relationships, taking toxic medicines, obesity, chronic stress, no loved or valued feeling, excessive negative stimuli, lousy posture, smoking, or smoke exposure, insufficient time outside, etc.

The direct result of an industrialized, "advanced" culture is so many of our unhealthy and dysfunctional lifestyles. It is difficult to argue that we are "advanced" in health and wellness, given our "advanced" efforts to address these issues, in all age groups, when the number of chronic diseases rises dramatically.

The rocks are sinking us painfully. There is a cumulative effect on everyone's health. We may not notice at first. Finally, we should understand that our daily lives have become more complicated and more difficult. They often don't even know how or when this happened.

On the planet, there is no drug that can remove the rocks for you! That is why it is not competent to treat the symptoms or the consequences of those rocks when it comes to addressing the real problem. The drugs will simply become another toxic block. (Listen just to the side effects on any drug commercial!) The removal of parts of the body is not much more comfortable to solve the problem. Because of a lack of medication or too many body parts, we're not sinking! The body is not' stupid.' This shows a completely normal physiological response to an environmental stressor.

The rocks have a different effect on your overall health. As more stone is applied to your backpack and you sink down, the pressure on your water wings rises, and the air flows faster. You lose your life more quickly than you originally planned. You age faster. You age quicker.

Such incongruous decisions or stressors in lifestyle are the catalysts for chronic disease. Such toxic and harmful choices lead to our so-called allostatic load.

The persistent allostatic strain of our genetic expression of the cellular function, physiology genetics, entire internal environment, eventually of health changes over months and years of inconsistent lifestyle choices. That's how chronic disease evolves.

It becomes evident that removing rocks from your backpack will help restore fitness, reducing the pressure on your water wings!

In the end, this means reducing our harmful and bad choices while maximizing pure and adequate decisions. It affects our climate and changes genetic expression. This is the study of epigenetics- how our nature influences our genetic code expression.

Fortunately, science showed us the strategy. We know what choices are leading us to health. We can solve that problem. The most successful way of meeting our inherent genetic requirements for health and wellness while avoiding chronic diseases is to follow a lifestyle close to our previous (and healthier) ancestors.

Tip to Bypass Chronic Illness

This tip deals with mindset and diet. Decide not to sulk about not having the opportunity to eat what you want. When you take a safe and rational approach effectively, you are at the forefront of your quest for aging without chronic disease. This is because fresh food is your body's primary source of energy. You really protect your body from aging with the incurable illness when you make beneficial food choices.

You can comfortably concentrate on your positive attitude in order to stay well for the rest of your life.

You only learn if you are unable to eat to support your overall health and, therefore, the ability to experience healthy well-being. The attitude is very personal and resides on your being's spiritual level.

Evaluate your approach to dust your old food beliefs.

You will then create new visions of aging and prepare to make real physical efforts. This is a significant beginning to fulfill your desire to show a lively, well-being body at any age.

Do you imagine life without respiratory problems, without bones and arthritis, with blocked sinuses and a feeling of satisfaction? Not to mention the doctor's bad news.

This is achievable for people with the right mindset and a health-care diet.

Let's look at an attitude instead of saying you are old enough to eat what you want to regard as your food paradox-you are aged, a good indicator that your body will not tolerate an unbalanced diet, such as a young person's eating vigilant style.

Another reason for this is that diseases such as colds, pains, or even a diagnosis of arthritis or a diabetes condition are both linked with an abundance of pure sugar and with a tendency to feed excessively on another food category-simple carbohydrates. Simple carbohydrates are contained in the pastries, juice drinks of 40 grams of sugar per collection, overwhelming starchy foods such as white potatoes in its various shapes, and white bread frequently served with foods high in saturated fat such as omnipresent burgers.

These are the diets of young people and teenagers, even for children. Nevertheless, the nutritional requirements necessary to maintain human cells at a healthy level have been deeply awakened. At this level, immune cells can play their protective role in preventing cancerous cells; they can sniff viral invaders away, and they have an army of cells that can dismantle allergies before they can sneeze.

This tip can be said quickly, but not easily done. You have to change your attitude. Take the confidence that fresh food will improve your wellbeing and recover. Decide now that you want to eat to satisfy your desire to be happy and good at any age. So believe it is possible for you, and you are on the road to positive aging.

Let's take your diet into account and eat out. Be particular about where you are eating and food quality as you age. Prepare to dine out. Plan eating out. In reality, this will tell you more about your plans to eat at home. Read more about the restaurants and preparation of their meals. List the places that you choose for the quality and the type of cooking you want for your new diet, for example, a fried meal should not be on your list only.

Then comes the moment of strength, when you revive your mind about food choices that can keep you healthy. Resolve your blood sugar control. Try to maintain the right level of blood sugar without drugs, but by making excellent food choices. Do not question that your body will continue to perform effectively to keep you happy and satisfied as you go through every stage of your life.

Drop your diet, weight loss quickly, and prepare to eat to maintain your health and body over your entire lifetime. This advice is more comfortable to say than to do.

But once you do this with particular enthusiasm, you will be surprised by how easy it is to maintain this attitude. Even with the scientific background, this is why people can have real access to healthy eating guidelines while shifting an eating model. Since food is mostly pure, naturally administered chemistry, it is even more amazing than your doctor's prescription. You can only determine whether you want to make an effort to plan. Keep in mind that success at this stage will help keep you healthy, but above all, an immune system that works well, whose role is to preserve your appearance, look, and feel beautiful.

HEALTHY LIFESTYLE TIPS

As a parent and breadwinner, you and your family have a primary duty to be physically healthy and to prevent the lengthy and hideous list of chronic diseases you can suffer, including cancer, cardiovascular attack, strokes, organ failure, etc. Medical aid, life insurance, and chronic disease cover may provide you with the financial security you need, but can never afford to protect you. It's the simple things you can do to stay healthy. To you, your family and yours.

- Limit the intake of alcohol then stop smoking
- Exercise three days a week for at least 22 minutes.
- Drink plenty of water and drink no dietary beverages or any other soft drinks except diluted pure fruit juice.
- Avoid processed food-eat your food as close as possible to its original condition. For starters, eat a bowl of oats and not a cereal with a cup of sugar.
- Fats are primarily found in animal products: beef, milk, and eggs, avoid saturated fats.

- Eat different fruits and vegetables every day, preferably organic and cooked only lightly.
- Avoid red meat, eat lean chicken and fish instead.
- Avoid sugar and raising the salt intake.
- Eat a lot of almonds, legumes, peas, and grains.
- Always skip breakfast and eat regular small meals.

Remember that the food you eat can be your poison or medicine—it is your choice. Good health is within your control with the right food choices.

Good health is not about hitting your target weight or strengthening your gym muscles. Good health is a way of life that our children should be taught by example. It's about giving our bodies the strength they need and then consciously using them every day. Good health ensures that we can prevent disease. Good health promotes an active mind, attention, and focus. Finally, a healthy body is a balanced mind with a well-documented correlation between health, a sensible diet, and a good mood.

Mindful Ways To Make Life Better Again

The open secret to a life of anxiety and panic, turning into a life of peace and happiness starts to be more alert and conscious. The attitude we take towards our situation has a significant impact on our result. We actually delude ourselves if we do not know how important our behavior is. Our actions are like magnets that attract us in similar ways. You heard the saying: garbage in, waste out. If we want to make life better again, we must stop fighting our present situation. The simple fact is that we lose every time we go to war with ourselves.

At the end of this novel, you see how important it is to see how certain behaviors trap you in the anxiety you don't want. We will also describe the initial reactions that lead you to what you want-overcoming all forms of anxiety.

This is all about turning unconscious habits into conscious habits that heal.

Let's just jump in: here are the positive ways to make life enjoyable again.

- Accept your current situation to resolve it. This must be the foundation upon which your entire recovery is founded. Acceptance is the foundation of every worthy endeavor-and what could be more important than the objective of mental and emotional welfare?

If we don't acknowledge where we really are, we simply add more negative energy to where we are heading. Indeed, at first, it's not easy to accept what we really don't want, especially as we are conditioned to resist what we don't want.

If we see, however, that what we resist persists, we can decide to work in harmony with and allow the law of our experience to be as it is. Accepting what is now, though looking at the end goal, really leads to FREE.

Support and be free or deny and jail. This is your choice. This is your preference.

- Many people believe that asking for assistance is a sign of weakness. Seek appropriate support without reluctance, guilt, or shame. In fact, it's the opposite. A genuinely humble person needs to be wise enough to ask for help. It takes a person with true humility to recognize that everyone has challenges throughout their lives; this is what you do with those challenges that make a difference.

Give somebody the opportunity to support you. If you find it hard to shake off feelings of guilt or humiliation, try to find help. They are just thoughts that stand in the way of your recovery. You can wait forever if you wait until you feel comfortable asking for support.

You can only feel more anxious by thinking about what others think about you. Therefore, one day you are in a position of strength and well-being and return the favor. We are here. No man is an island, are we not?

Be strong and seek the assistance you need.

- How many times do we remember laughing at something that we thought at first wasn't funny? What has it done to your feelings? Has it not taken away most (if not all) of its power over you?

If you look closer, in a not-so-funny situation, you can always find something funny. It's very close to finding the silver belt in any case-if you look for it, and it will be there. This does not mean taking the situation lightly but instead seeing the light in your case.

Laughter has an accurate way to decrease your anxiety significantly. If your situation doesn't reveal the humor, watch a funny film, read a funny book, or listen to your favorite comic. Consider hanging out with lighter people than you, but make sure that these people really care for you.

- If we make unrealistic predictions or half-empty assumptions about our chances of recovery, we effectively close the door to our willingness to see our condition as it is. We close the door to our ability to recognize that we are far more than transient situations.

Wonder and curiosity affect our emotional state in such a neutralizing and soothing way. We're prepared and open to the healing that we really desire when we don't draw conclusions as to how' hopeless' our condition is or worry of all the hard work it will take' to overcome anxiety.

It is simply not possible to talk enough about staying in wonder, curiosity, and openness. Even if you look to live a happy and complete life, it's yours to collect. You can't heal yourself, but you can treat yourself.

- Asking the right questions reveals the correct answers. Either we face the direction of our cure at any moment, or we face more fear and anxiety. Ask questions such as,' Why are you so weak? And' Why does that happen to me? It's only about bringing you down, keeping you stuck in what you don't want. It's like walking in stable sand if you could stop it by walking on solid ground.

Ask questions such as,' What specific things do you stop in order to improve? and.' How can you make the best possible day today? Two big questions got you looking in the right direction.

What are you in your situation funny about? and.' What do you usually take for granted, thank you?

These are questions that inspire and focus our attention on the path of our cure.

The right questions have a reorienting impact. If we are in self-doubt or unnecessary anxiety, an inspiring question can be asked to shift our attention and energy quickly.

- When we unconsciously focus on what we would not want, we get more of what we don't want. Focus on what we don't want. This is a fundamental and straightforward concept, which never takes sides or plays favorites. Angst and phobia sufferers tend to concentrate on the negative towards the maximum—and then wonder why all this stress doesn't seem to go anywhere.

If an archer wants to land his arrow right in the middle of the bull's eye, then he will surely block out all else and go to the bull's eye center. It's no different. We must be mindful of where the power and attention are focused because we will definitely get what we concentrate on.

We must be conscious enough to concentrate and focus actively on what we want, not what we don't want. Sure that after night you concentrate on that which you don't like, you get more than that which you don't want. Concentrate on what you want.

- No doubt, you have heard or read that the key to living a fulfilled life is to be thankful. And honestly, it can be irritating, particularly if your life doesn't feel like grateful. What do you mean thank you? How can you be thankful if you think that you lose your mind?

How can you be thankful if you cannot even draw the courage to put aside your fears and concerns to leave the place to shop for food? Congratulations are due to those who have a good life, and to those who are happy and content, right?

Always focus on everything that is wrong or missing is a great way to stay trapped in a life you don't want. Turn your focus to everything you admire for inspiring you to take the steps towards full recovery. If you find this difficult, you will begin to be grateful that you are alive!

When we spend most of the day dictating negative thoughts and attitudes, we will not conquer fear so quickly. Thankfully, when we wallow in the victim's mindset, we have the capacity to shift our attention from the negative to the positive automatically.

The fight against anxiety, panic, social phobia, agoraphobia, and OCD must not be a long, painful, and drawn-out process. It can be a relatively short period in your life—and in your rearview mirror, you can have it earlier than later, if you consciously adopt the attitudes leading to recovery.

Even in a country with such advanced healthcare, like the US, these conditions are often disregarded and continue to strike people if they are the most vulnerable. Studies show that 60 percent more prevalent anxiety disorders are in women than in men, which is an enormous downside for so many women today as adult life is on the verge of anxiety.

All have the potential to accumulate once in the context of an individual and are but an example of how stress and anxiety act on a person. We often live our lives without being aware of the smallest wounds to our mental health every day.

What Leads to Be the Man or Anxious Constant Assessment The world today is natural to be washed over by how many people actually assess their acts every day. There is, of course, space for exaggeration, but the fact is that so many people focus on how others do it and only judge it by what they see. You are judged on the basis of your appearance, voice, way of doing things, gesticulation based on relationships and interactions, often also based on your context, mother tongue, degrees, and most often what others think about yourself. People rarely approach other people without any preconceived notions, and this creates a sound basis for stereotyping.

We are separated and put in these mental boxes that people create for ourselves and for our potential. All this happens without you even beginning real interaction with the judge, but we were all culpable of that at some point in our lives. Analyzing how the process is handled by your own brain can be the key to understanding what lies behind our evaluation of others. First of all, you relate the attributes of another person to what they had to do during your past experiences. This is achieved so quickly that you only consider the implications—the same thing that happens when your memories reappear. It may be compared to how Windows downloads and installs the updates when you can see every three-hundredth of thousands of them, which are not verified yet but the life that you seldom have encountered.

In fact, the roots of your assessment are placed in almost the same soil as your memories, since any preconceived notion is that the mind in action is reappearing. You store ties between the facial expressions of people and their attitude towards life or towards you, the connections between the role of people and their acts, between the voice tone of people and their treatment of others. There are thousands of these links for every brain, and irrespective of how narrow-minded they seem these days, it has once been vital for human survival.

Since the advent of our species, we have lived in communities that strive to obtain food and shelter, and as we have all witnessed once-when demand is more significant than supply, conflict is generated. Wasn't the language really a diplomatic thing back then? Forget about it. People had to rely on other sources of information to determine the danger in which they were-whether another person wanted to attach to their tribe or to destroy their neighbors. An expression, the way one used to say which chain of events may happen. Make no mistake-your risk assessment methods are still tremendous help, but in so many situations, we seem to get too far with how much we can derive from a person's appearance. Very few men and women today understand this, take a closer look at gossip, and how often one human being can shape and exchange preconceptions with another.

Do not get overwhelmed if you feel you're being assessed if you have a judicious eye-just realize that you've been guilty of a similar act once, and think about what that means.

The collapse of a friendship or relationship, the death of a significant person can often become a trauma for the remainder of your life. At the next moment, you believe that all your values will be shattered by that one incident, and profound doubt and worry will begin to take over. This even strengthens the trauma in so many cases, causing you to experience pain in almost excessive quantities.

The truth is that irrespective of how painful the encounter is, your life after that is driven by your thoughts that–in the emotional baggage you bear – never function as a support to relieve your suffering. You tend to relive what happened as if it never ended and get caught in a vortex of uncontrollable thinking. It often contributes to disorders such as PTSD (Post-Traumatic Stress Disorder), which alone affects 25 million people in the United States. Perhaps if we were adequately educated on how to handle these sometimes life-changing events, could all this be avoided.

Those with PTSD never even know they have established a disability and have no hope of changing their lives. We are trapped in the present and dread any step forward because we feel like they can witness an incident that is somewhat like their past.

Social pressures for decades, people have been trying to focus attention on how many stresses our culture and society is putting on every human being. This differs dramatically across the globe, but their profound effect cannot be avoided. You are built on standards set by the culture of your parents, and you develop habits that fit where you grew up, rebel against what you have as a member of society, and you very often end up making peace, where you have come from—burying the hatchet. In most cases, these community enforcements have minimal effect on what is relevant to you, but sometimes you are caught up in the rules of the region as often what is decided by the majority is far from what is right. Note that slavery used to be the norm.

Social pressures are very similar in nature to the previously discussed pre-conceptions because what was once associated by some citizens is forbidden or forced upon. When some people agree about the fairness of something, it becomes a precedent for every new member of their social group, without even making them conscious of how to behave.

Striving for excellence Springing from the social pressures described above is often the search for perfection that so many of us know about. In the vast majority of cases, we have an ideal-when you're a boy, your parents, once you go to school, they come from your teachers, then you and your employers start imposing it on your own sons and daughters at a certain level. People sometimes justify their need for excellence by referring to their inspiration, but this is only a bunch of BS. You can, of course, do everything you can to do your utmost, but the details–generally unnoticeable to an untrained eye–are an exaggeration — a very harmful one. Perfection, in its essence, is unachievable-a slight flaw will always be noticed.

CHAPTER FIVE

Overcoming Anxiety

Overcoming anxiety as a typical anxiety disorder patient can be a challenge. Although it is considered normal that people are somewhat anxious to some degree, a person with a Generalized Anxiety Disorder has little to no anxiety relief. Sufferers of this condition also experience chronic anxiety, constant concerns, and high levels of pressure, and there is typically no clear explanation for this stress. If you suffer from this disorder, you will learn some steps to conquer anxiety in this guide.

There are many different symptoms that can be encountered if a person suffers from Generalizing Anxiety Disorder. Symptoms of Generalized Anxiety Disorder Regrettably, the overcome of fears caused by these symptoms often reaches such a high level with all signs that the standard anxiety relief techniques are ineffective.

- High levels of worry about a wide range of personal issues

- Experience high levels of restlessness and failure to experience anxiety relief

- Periods of loss in attention and memory levels

- Mood changes that may include anger, depression, and irritability when managing anxiety are not effective

- Respiratory complementation.

Overcoming Anxiety Successfully: If a person suffers from this disorder, the main objective is to learn strategies to overcome anxiety. In some cases, medication and therapy sessions may determine a reason for the disease. No cause can be identified in other cases. In some cases, the symptoms associated with Generalized Anxiety Disorder stem directly from imbalances in the body related to neurotransmitters, hormones, and other chemicals.

If you are suffering from this disorder and are looking for anxiety relief, consider:

- Some drugs may be used to relieve anxiety. Usually, **GAD** patients are treated for antidepressants, anti-anxiety medications, and sedatives. All these have proven to be effective in managing stress.

- Most anxiety sufferers seek the help of psychotherapy trained professionals. This form of treatment recognizes stressors in the life of an anxiety seeker and assists with behavioral changes so that circumstances which the mind and body perceive to be a "danger" are better addressed. Some agree that this is a positive way to overcome anxiety.

- If you are depressed and engage in drug abuse or smoking to relieve anxiety, it is essential to understand that this can just intensify the stress. If you have a problem with drug addiction, seeking help will help you overcome fear right away.

- Relaxation techniques become increasingly popular when anxiety is overcome. Such methods can include simple exercises, music therapy, listening, and even yoga.

- Intake of healthy foods can be an essential anxiety management technique.

It can be difficult to overcome anxiety linked to Generalized Anxiety Disorder, but it is not impossible. You can find some degree of anxiety relief by using the technique described here. When you find that you cannot succeed in managing fear, it might be necessary to seek an expert's advice.

You can't overcome fear by going to the center of stress reduction in your lifetime. Unless you obviously want anxiety relief, you will have to take control of everything that induces stress and anxiety in your life.

In some lives, fear goes far beyond tension and anxiety. Often anxiety gets severe and can even lead to panic attacks. You are likely to find ways to alleviate stress in your life if you have ever developed this condition.

The key to managing anxiety starts with understanding. You have to know what, how, and even why, to some degree, to treat or cure something. Perhaps learning more about an anxiety-like condition goes a long way to the symptoms, so you know exactly what you are facing.

What is the condition of anxiety?

Anxiety disorder varies in severity and nature from regular anxiety. Everyone is very interested in their lives, but when this becomes obsessive or overwhelming, a good chance of anxiety disorder or panic attacks is the root cause.

Your worries and feelings are the same things as many others, but if you are nervous, you will hit an entirely new level of concern. For example, if you call a friend and your appeal is not returned immediately, you start to agonize about the relationship and wonder what's wrong.

How or why, there is evidence that panic attacks and anxiety are legacies. The only question is whether this influence is inherited or merely the natural condition tendency from living with a terrifying parent. Nevertheless, studies have demonstrated that children who live with anxiety-ridden parents are more likely than other children to develop affliction.

You may be shocked when looking for ways to resolve fear to learn that panic disorders are often linked to timidity. Individuals also who have never stood up or are desperately trying to make peace need a way out of these feelings that have accumulated over many years and may have been in a panic attack or anxiety problem.

Overcoming Whatever the cause and effect relationship is, one thing is usually in the mind of the patient the way to overcome anxiety. There some ways to do this, and one or more of them may be very beneficial. Most of the time, fear is resolved by combined actions.

Medication can be prescribed by the doctor to relieve anxiety. In general, you are put on either an anti-depressant or tranquilizer-type drug. Most doctors are wary of the first type of medication because of the high risk of abuse and addiction. Anti-depressants can be beneficial, but take a while to get into the system and work.

Cognitive-behavioral therapy is one of the best ways to overcome anxiety and panic attacks. This practice involves a licensed therapist who will guide you through new thinking and behavioral changes. This can be achieved with various methods like aversion.

It is essential that you find a way to conquer anxiety and panic in your life. Your family will benefit, but above all, you can again find joy in life. You can also prevent more severe complications, such as agoraphobia, anxiety, and panic attacks.

It is almost impossible to overcome anxiety without getting to the heart of that stress in your life. If you want to feel natural anxiety relief, you need to take control of everything that induces fear and anxiety in your life.

Overcoming Anxiety With No Medication

More and more anxiety patients do not use medicine to overcome anxiety. Here you will find out why diet is one of the most successful ways of helping to overcome anxiety disorder. First of all, let us investigate why more and more anxieties turn from pharmaceutical drugs to natural ways to overcome their fear.

The common drugs a doctor prescribes are antidepressants to help regulate the mood, calm down, and beta-blockers that help control the physical symptoms of anxiety and anxiety.

And these can work well if administered correctly and accompanied by the patient's note. So why do so many people refuse rather than taking anxiety medicines? Mainly because of their severe side effects, dependency problems in some cases are included. And because these drugs don't work for everyone, too.

Do not stop taking anxiety medication without first consulting the doctor. When you encounter any adverse side effects from your prescription drug, go to the doctor immediately and speak to him about the issue. To help overcome anxiety in natural ways, the aim is to reduce your stress and anxiety as much as possible. Already, you would think it is difficult if you are suffering from general anxiety and perhaps frequent anxiety attacks. And it might be. But you can take natural steps to help you do this.

And your diet is one of the most essential and healthy things.

The trick is to use a healthy diet for fatigue relief, hydration, and the buildup of your autoimmune system, etc. Poor diets do the reverse and can make managing the general anxiety very difficult. Here are a few essential dietary steps to conquer fear.

- Stay well hydrated with a total of 12x 8 of glasses of water per day. Drink 100% natural fruit juices.

- Make sure you eat many fruit and vegetables.

- Eat meat sparingly, just enough to provide ample fat and protein.

- Use plenty of complex carbohydrates (Pommes of potatoes, pasta, wheat, etc.) to regulate the blood sugar.

- Check for enough fatty acids (tuna, fish oils, salmon, etc.) as there is evidence that insufficient fatty acids may cause anxiety and depression.

Please consider taking additional natural products to make up for some of your diet's essential vitamins, minerals, and nutrients.

Eliminate caffeine, for example vitamin B complex, vitamin E, etc.

As known, stimulants coffee, tea, chocolate, and fizzy drink, etc. should be avoided. At the very least, their intake is dramatically reduced. Avoid alcohol, which is calming for the first couple of drinks but can then serve as a higher intake depressant.

Note: If these are very drastic changes to your current diet, consult your doctor before introducing them now, while these dietary changes can be significant for helping you to reduce anxiety, there's another problem you need to address: this is the' fear factor.' So, once you have had a panic attack, what happens is that you're scared of another. The insecurity may be known in your subconscious or what it is.

In fact, this fear may build on your general anxiety in such a way that it can trigger an anxiety attack while fear of an attack can cause one! You will interrupt this anxiety loop so that anxiety attacks can be minimized and better placed to conquer the general anxiety.

Naturally Overcoming Anxiety

You faced the storm long enough. And or You have just come to understand that you are vulnerable to panic or anxiety. You would like some support. The great news is that it is not only possible to resolve anxiety attacks but very likely to be carried out by most people.

While you should still speak to your counselor or therapist if you are in real common or constant anxiety, you can do a great deal for yourself to resolve the anxiety attack. It involves changing a few ingrained habits, learning some new skills, and a bite of integrity, but it is undoubtedly worth the last product.

The reality is, it's a pleasurable experience for the most part because you start to feel better and better. We'll start with a few basics to get you on the right track. Such a few tips are crucial to building a strong base.

- Be truthful enough. Be frank enough. But the first step is to be honest because the reaction you have is triggering your fear or panic. Not a separate case. This does not mean that you might not need to reflect on some of the problems in your life; it mainly means that the way you respond to them is essential.

- Get enough sleep. Many people in our way of life are deprived of sleep. There are many punishments, but the starting point is that it worsens you and makes you less capable of coping with your life correctly. Adequate sleep requires choosing what is called "good sleep hygiene," rest before sleep, not eating or exercising too late, etc...

- Get some workout. You don't have to be turned into a marathon athlete. Just make sure you have some regular exercise. Even a stroll every day makes a huge difference. It's good for your body, good for your health and strength of mind. This makes you feel better and work healthier.

- Learn how to relax deliberately. Many people don't know how to relax, connect with relaxation, and unconsciousness. The truth though, is that learning to let go consciously and to return to a relaxed self knowingly is essential for overcoming anxiety attacks. It can be paired with diet, holiday with loved ones, or meditation work. You can even hear your favorite music, but the idea is to let yourself go and find your happy self consciously.

- A healthy lifestyle may undoubtedly include a nice cup of coffee in the morning or a glass of wine in the evening, but it is an indicator that something is out of order in which that caffeine, alcohol, or tobacco need to survive throughout the day. Stimulants can make us more nervous, and alcohol can only cover up underlying problems.

Of course, this is only the foundation because anxiety disorders can be arduous without a competent base. There's a lot that you can get out of when you are ready to regain your life.

Mindfulness Psychotherapy For Overcoming Anxiety

Attention is a type of conscious awareness in which we are fully aware of experience as it evolves. This may not sound different to our normal awareness perception, so we need to explore social awareness first to understand consciousness better. If we have an experience external to us, such as vision, sound or touch, or inner experiences, such as feelings, memory, or emotions, the mind tends to respond to the experience according to past conditioning. When we look at a tree, we not only see the tree as it is, but we see a composite of the objective reality of the tree and our subjective reality, which is our internal representation of the tree. We understand the results of our individual tree reactions, and this so frequently affects our vision and awareness that we can see very little of the reality of what lies before us.

We may define consciousness as a continuum from totally objective reality to a totally subjective reactivity on the one hand. Many of us are more personal than objective, and our perceptions are dominated by an individual habitual reactivity that blinds us to reality.

Consciousness is an attempt to correct this disparity and reduce typical subjective reactivity and transfer knowledge into the tactile experience. Consequently, mindfulness is often defined as direct awareness or the emphasis on present experience. It is a non-reactive consciousness that enables us to perceive every aspect of knowledge entirely. One of the best terms used to describe consumer perception is present. Pleasure allows us to be fully present with our experience as it is, rather than thinking about what we are doing, evaluating our knowledge, or responding with desire or dislike.

Consciousness is a hallmark of the Buddha's teachings and considers awareness to be the foundation necessary for interior transformation as well as the cleansing of body, speech, and mind actions described in the Noble Eightfold Path. Without first developing attention, a person can not perfect morality, compassion, and correct response; for conscience is the car for seeing the reality and truth of the things as they are rather than distorted by our prejudices and beliefs.

The Buddha made it very clear in connection with the mind that if you want to change inner emotional suffering, you have to open the eye to the mind and look in to see what is there. Thinking and Reactivity take you away from this primary and direct perception because you experience the response, not the original object when you react. If you find your fear or depression, you know that your target is not the same as the primary emotion. You are taken away by reactivity, which really is a subtle type of suppression, and if the mind is ignored by any kind of destruction, it is stopped from changing.

The first prerequisite to transform anxiety is that you can experience it thoroughly, be fully present, and be mindful of the emotion. Nothing can change without this effort to overcome unconsciousness. In reality, ignorance is an essential factor which, first of all, creates anxiety. This is especially the case for depression in which the central emotional or trauma has a complex superstructure of negative reactive thought. The first aspect or element of mindfulness is, therefore, the active watchful portion, which is called Recognition or Vigilance. We train ourselves to recognize every reactivity move in mind so that we can stop its proliferation and become conscious of the core emotions.

Attention, however, is multi-dimensional. It is not just learning to be more mindful but to move from a piece of fundamental knowledge to a relationship of total presence, in which you look and listen with a calm, quiet mind. The second dimension of perception is how you respond to the central emotion or any other sensation you have. Mindfulness is like a light that enlightens the excitement and keeps the mind on the excitement. This stops passion from being diverted. Now, we must continue to shine a light on the emotion and start the process of careful research.

Carefulness enables us to establish a spacious, non-threatening, and safe relationship with our inner emotional complexes. We are so used to responding that we never spend any time with our emotions. It's like a crazy friend who never seems to have time for a cup. "This is what we are doing all the time with our emotional suffering; we are not just taking the time to be present with our inner misery, and it is hardly shocking that the pain continues. Attention is everything about making time to be with your emotions, literally sitting with it and listening as you do with a friend. The second dimension of focus is, therefore, PRESENCE and RELATIONSHIP. Everybody all understands how essential it is to be fully present when they struggle with your spouse or relative. You need more than advice or words in your presence.

After you have developed your identity, the third dimension of consciousness arises very naturally, and that is an INVESTIGATION. If we observe an emotion like anxiety or depression with focus, it reacts by differentiating into subtler emotions, memories, and inner imagination. We actually see more, and that is very necessary since this transformation becomes a probability in the specifics of what we see. Like a car that doesn't start, the best answer is to remove the cap and look inside the engine.

Solutions are provided. If you see a wire lose, the solution is straightforward; but first, you had to look in, or you never found the answer. We still remain stuck in the superficial appearance of our emotions; we find our anxiety or depression to be strong forces, when they are rarely firm and never what they seem to be first. The excitement is like a wall, and the process of taking out bricks and mortar is a consciousness. Once you start dismantling the anger, the ideas begin to appear very randomly.

There is, therefore, the fourth dimension of focus, a **TRANSFORMATIONAL** environment. We learn not to respond first, and then we learn to be present. As we are present, the inner structure of the emotion is revealed, and this paves the way for transformation. Each of these new measures of understanding is revolutionary, but effective psychotherapy stands for overcoming reactivity and learning to respond to inner pain. Nonetheless, making our depression's internal structure-aware will lead directly to change at the core level.

The mind has an incredible ability to repair itself when it has the freedom to change, and consciousness allows this independence. We all have intrinsic inner knowledge of wisdom, which is called satipanna. This translates from chaos to peace, from conflict to harmony and from misery to happiness. This natural intelligence, which constantly changes to maintain health, is like the experience of the body called homeostasis. Psychological homeostasis also drives the mind to health and happiness. When consciousness is established, we create the ideal conditions of inner liberty in which this natural intelligence directs the internal transformation process.

CONCLUSION

Often people are still uncertain about the causes of depression. A split with the loved one, health problems, loss of a family member, and even financial difficulties are some of the probable causes of depression. Of reality, these things are terrible when they are encountered. In general, a person tends to give in only to depression. That's not the way, though. Depression can be resolved for everyone. Although it is evident that there is no quick response to depression, it is still feasible.

Everything, not even depression, is permanent. It's not a do-or-die stance. And you don't have to lift your finger to conquer depression. And once you finally overcome your depression, you're going to know how to try something new and enjoyable. You wouldn't have to live in the dark and force yourself to recover every moment of poverty.

Many people are still uncertain about the real cause of depression. The general idea is that you are depressed by a present sorrowful situation. But this is not the case in reality. Which makes a person sad is the fact that you dwell too much on the unfortunate situation you are in. It's an awkward stage, in fact, but it doesn't stop the world. You ought to start with your life.

Depression is a hazardous trap. You know why? It's because if you fall in depression and pay full attention to negative things, you can be likened to a person in fast sand. You can't even find any ways to overcome stress, such as anti-depressants or therapy. Depressed people are using temporary relief strategies, such as opioids, alcohol, or anything, which can only make them more conscious. Such forms of interim relief are definitely not productive. Unfortunately, it can even make things worse. If you want to overcome your depression, you cannot continue running from problems.

So what is the correct solution to resolve depression if these things don't work? It's not a natural way.

Yes, it is apparent that you don't have to raise your finger to do so. It's not, though, what people expect. The real answer to overcoming your depression is to minimize the attention you offer to the negative thing, place, or case. It's not about running away from your problems. The problem is to focus on good things in life's happiness. Yes, it is advantageous when you are free from depression. When you consistently lift and stop thinking about bad things in your life, any sort of depression will undoubtedly vanish from you. This is only possible when you spend more time on something to make you happy.